MOTOR RACING PUBLICATIONS LIMITED
Unit 6, The Pilton Estate, 46 Pitlake, Croydon CR0 3RY, England

First published 1995

British Library Cataloguing in Publication Data
Taylor, James
  Choosing A Used 4x4: The Essential Buyer's Guide to Off-Road
  Vehicles
  I. Title
  629.22042
ISBN 0-947981-96-9

Publisher's note:
Multi-purpose vehicles have a higher centre of gravity and different steering/handling characteristics from ordinary road cars. Your driving technique will need adapting accordingly.

Typesetting and origination by
Keele University Press, Staffordshire
Printed in Great Britain by The Amadeus Press Ltd,
Huddersfield, West Yorkshire

Contents

Page

Introduction

The main aim of this book is to provide a ready reference guide for anyone who is planning to buy a 4x4 vehicle for recreational or daily use, or for a combination of the two. One of the great advantages of today's four-wheel drive vehicles is that so many of them really are dual-purpose machines, able to serve as everyday transport during the week and for off-road fun at the weekends.

However, this book does not pretend to be a guide to every off-road vehicle on the British market today. It does not cover commercial vehicles, but concentrates specifically on those vehicles which are intended primarily to carry passengers. As the great boom in the passenger-carrying 4x4 market occurred in the Eighties, it does not deal with vehicles which went out of production before the beginning of that decade. Similarly, it would be quite impractical to include all the most recently introduced models and derivatives because more and more new 4x4s are being announced all the time and it would therefore be impossible to be right up to date; however, as the book is intended mainly to help buyers of a used vehicle, those which are too new to be available in any quantity secondhand have not been covered in detail.

Two Land Rovers and a Range Rover, two Vauxhall Fronteras and a Ford Maverick – a typical cross-section of the 4x4 vehicles seen in action one wet afternoon at the David Bowyer Off-Road Centre in Devon.

Why four-wheel drive?

The Eighties saw a great surge of interest in four-wheel drive vehicles for everyday use. As a result most of the major manufacturers now have products in this area of the market, which used to be a specialist preserve. A look at the history of four-wheel drive vehicles (see below) provides some explanations for this change, but it is also interesting to see what perceptions underpin the genre's current popularity.

There are four main reasons why customers buy four-wheel drive vehicles in the mid-Nineties. The first is associated with *safety*. In an age when crash safety has become a major preoccupation, the size and perceived strength of a four-wheel drive vehicle are important factors in its appeal. So is the knowledge that having all four wheels driven provides better roadholding in poor weather conditions than having just the front or rear pair driven.

The second reason is that four-wheel drive vehicles represent *fun* – and in a variety of ways. Buyers of stylish short-wheelbase vehicles often see them as the visible expression of the active sporting lifestyle to which they aspire or already enjoy. Soft-top models which can be used with the top down in good weather in particular demonstrate that driving from A to B can be enjoyable as well as functional.

Neither of these elements is really relevant to the long-wheelbase 'family' 4x4s – although some of them are designed to resemble their more carefree smaller sisters – but the element of off-road ability is common to all 4x4s. The truth is that the vast majority of 4x4 owners never take their vehicles into really rough terrain, so never discover their vehicles' true capabilities. However, off-road driving is widely acknowledged to be an enjoyable activity, and there is a subliminal element of "I could if I wanted to" in the reasons for purchasing a 4x4. A similar underlying thought motivates many people to buy cars capable of very high speeds which they may not even approach legally and probably never will approach in reality.

A third reason why four-wheel drives are popular is that they are perceived as *different* – although this motivation for purchase must be on the decline as increasingly more 4x4 vehicles take to the roads. The short-wheelbase 4x4 certainly is different from the hot hatchback saloon from which many owners graduate – although some manufacturers have tried to minimize the differences – and the long-wheelbase family 4x4 certainly is different from the typical alternative of a Volvo or Ford Granada saloon-based estate. Manufacturers have exploited this element of being different by promoting 4x4s as the embodiment of rugged individualism, and on the back of that they have introduced profitable ranges of accessories to individualize or personalize a vehicle.

All of these factors contribute to the fourth principal reason why buyers choose a four-wheel drive: *image*. The image associated with a four-wheel drive vehicle is made up of a number of elements. There is strength, ruggedness and size, all of which may be interpreted as a reflection of the way the owner would like to be seen. There is the carefree lifestyle element associated particularly with the short-wheelbase soft-top models. It would probably not be fanciful to suggest that the rise of the four-wheel drive rally car in the Eighties added its own sporting spice to the image of a road-going four-wheel drive vehicle. And lastly, there is the individualism which allows the owner to believe he or she really is an individual rather than an anonymous face in the traffic jam.

4x4 characteristics

Most modern cars have monocoque construction, where engine, suspension and other components are all attached directly to the rigid steel box which forms the body. However, the majority of 4x4s have a separate chassis and body, the former usually a ladder-frame type with box-section sidemembers and a number of crossmembers. This provides additional strength for rough-terrain work, but also adds three or four inches to the overall height of the vehicle simply because the body sits on top of it.

4x4s also have drive to all four wheels instead of to the front or rear pair, as in most cars. This is designed to improve traction for difficult terrain, and it also improves traction on the road. However, the extra drivetrain components needed can increase fuel consumption and noise, so many 4x4s have selectable four-wheel drive, in which drive to one axle (usually the front) can be disengaged for road use. This is often supplemented by freewheeling front hubs, which allow the wheels to rotate independently of the axle driveshafts and thus reduce mechanical drag and noise. Freewheeling front hubs are engaged either manually (usually by a large knob in the wheel centres) or automatically (when four-wheel drive is selected).

Traditional to 4x4s used in rough terrain is a transfer gearbox, which is located between the primary gearbox and the propeller shafts to the axles. It has two gearsets: the High range is normally used for road driving and the Low range, which gears down the output from the primary gearbox, is engaged to give crawler gears for off-road work. Four-wheel drive is also manually selected through the transfer box in vehicles with selectable four-wheel drive systems.

Some 4x4s have differential locks for really tough going. A differential is designed to allow wheels on the same axle to rotate at different speeds, as they must during cornering, but it also allows power to go to the wheel with less resistance. Off-road, this will result in the vehicle being immobilized, as all power will go to a wheel which is spinning uselessly off the ground while none goes to the opposite wheel which has ground contact. To prevent that, a differential lock is provided: when it is engaged, power is distributed evenly to both wheels and thus the one with ground contact will propel the vehicle forward.

Vehicles with permanent four-wheel drive also have centre differentials, to allow their front and rear axles to rotate at different speeds. These differentials can have the same effect as an axle differential off-road, when power will be transferred to an axle where both wheels are spinning and none will go to the

Some people may dismiss off-roading as motorsport for masochists, but the ever-increasing popularity of the activity should silence the cynics. Even for the complete novice there are numerous specialist driving centres where skills can be taught by experts and developed in safety.

axle which has ground contact. Centre differential locks are provided to overcome this problem.

Tyres are a very important element of a 4x4's make-up. Those which give quiet running and predictable grip on the road very often do not have a sufficiently aggressive tread to claw their way through soft going off-road. Conversely, tyres with the best tread pattern for off-road use are noisy on the road and do not give the best roadholding. Most 4x4s are fitted with compromise types which are biased towards road use. Few drivers exceed the limits of these tyres off the road, but those who want to take their mud-plugging activities seriously are well advised to take professional advice and to buy a second set of wheels and tyres for off-road use.

How to use this book

The entry for each vehicle or group of vehicles is divided into a number of sections. First comes a *Background* section, which gives an overview of the vehicle and its origins. Next come its *Vital statistics*, or specifications, which include towing weights (maximum braked), fuel consumption and road performance figures. Sections entitled *Character summary* and *Performance summary* give an idea of what the vehicle is like to live with and how it behaves both on and off the road. *Reliability, weaknesses, spares* gives warnings where warnings are needed and reassurance where they are not. *Key specification changes in the UK* provides dates of major changes – which have not always been the same in the UK as in other markets. *Nomenclature* is a guide to the often confusing array of model-names associated with each range of vehicles, and *Resale values* gives an indication as to whether a vehicle is likely to prove a good investment in the longer term.

Lastly, *Club information* includes details of owners' clubs where appropriate (but contact details can change, so it is advisable to cross-check in magazines devoted to off-road vehicles), and *Further reading* gives references to full road tests by the leading British motoring magazines. Copies of these tests can be obtained from the magazines' publishers, at the following addresses:

Autocar and Motor (also *Autocar*)
38–42 Hampton Road
Teddington
Middlesex TW11 0JE

Diesel Car
Merricks Publishing Ltd
4 Wessex Buildings
Bancombe Road Trading Estate
Somerton
Somerset TA11 6SB

International Off-Roader
Milebrook Ltd
Anglian House
Chapel Lane
Botesdale
Diss
Norfolk IP22 1DT

Land Rover Owner
EMAP National Publications Ltd
Bushfield House
Orton Centre
Peterborough PE2 5UW

Land Rover World
Link House Magazines Ltd
Dingwall Avenue
Croydon
Surrey CR9 2TA

Motor
(see *Autocar and Motor*)

Off Road and 4 Wheel Drive
Link House Magazines Ltd
Dingwall Avenue
Croydon
Surrey CR9 2TA

Vehicle categories
There are several different categories of passenger-carrying 4x4, and buyers interested in one type may have very little interest in any others. Before purchasing a 4x4, it is also advisable to be very clear about what you intend to use it for because this will have a considerable impact on your choice.

For convenience, the vehicles covered in this book are listed below according to category; in the main body of the book they are listed in alphabetical order. Here, as throughout the rest of the book, SWB stands for short-wheelbase models (usually with three doors) and LWB for long-wheelbase types (usually with five doors).

Weekend fun and young image 4x4s
Asia Rocsta
Dacia Duster

Daihatsu Fourtrak SWB
Daihatsu Sportrak
Ford Maverick SWB
Isuzu Trooper SWB (first and second generations)
Jeep Wrangler
Lada Niva
Mahindra Jeep
Mercedes-Benz G-Wagen SWB (Soft Top)
Mitsubishi Shogun SWB (first and second generations)
Nissan Patrol SWB (first and second generations)
Nissan Terrano II SWB
Suzuki SJ410, SJ413, Santana and Samurai
Suzuki Vitara SWB
Toyota Land Cruiser II
Toyota RAV-4
Vauxhall Frontera Sport (SWB)

Utility passenger 4x4s
Nissan Patrol LWB (first and second generations)
Toyota Land Cruiser LWB (first generation, early models)
UMM Alter (Standard and LWB)

Family 4x4s
Daihatsu Fourtrak LWB
Ford Maverick LWB
Isuzu Trooper LWB (first and second generations)
Jeep Cherokee
Land Rover 88 and 109 County
Land Rover 90 County and Defender 90 County
Land Rover 110 County and Defender 110 County
Land Rover Discovery
Mercedes-Benz G-Wagen SWB
Mercedes-Benz G-Wagen LWB (earlier models)
Mitsubishi Shogun LWB (first and second generations)
Nissan Terrano II LWB
Suzuki Vitara LWB
Toyota Land Cruiser LWB (first generation, later models)
Toyota Land Cruiser VX (LWB, second generation)
Toyota 4-Runner
Vauxhall Frontera Estate (LWB)
Vauxhall Monterey

Luxury 4x4s
Range Rover
Mercedes-Benz G-Wagen LWB (later models)
Mitsubishi Shogun LWB (second generation, some models)

Some Range Rovers may be called upon to tackle nothing more hazardous than the King's Road, Chelsea, but this luxurious 4x4 is no mean performer when taken off-road.

Common appraisal points

There is no need here to discuss all the points to consider when looking over a used road vehicle prior to purchase, but there are certain additional points which apply to 4x4s. First of all, 4x4s are designed to be used off the road, and some certainly will have been. Although their design allows them to take the strain without difficulty, it is still possible for a driver to do some damage if he or she gets into difficulties off-road. The tell-tale signs of heavy off-roading are likely to be caked mud in the engine bay and on the vehicle's lower parts (some always clings in the crevices, even if the vehicle has been cleaned). If these signs are present, make a special check for dented chassis rails and damage to the underside of the vehicle.

Many people buy 4x4s because they make good tow vehicles, and once again most examples are built to stand the strain. The obvious sign that a vehicle has been used for towing is a tow hitch at the rear. Try to find out what it has towed: caravans are unlikely to have caused any problems, but overloaded trailers can put a lot of strain on the clutch and transmission, so double-check these areas for trouble.

The spacious rear quarters of many 4x4s also means that they are often bought by people who use them for carrying large dogs and sometimes other animals. That in itself is no problem – unless there are residual smells – but animals of all kinds can rapidly damage upholstery if left unattended to roam around the inside of a vehicle. Some 4x4s are therefore likely to show evidence of this, so bargain accordingly.

Personalizing a vehicle by means of accessories is part of 4x4 culture, and the makers pander to it mercilessly. A basic vehicle can, of course, be equipped with accessories such as air conditioning or anti-lock brakes in exactly the same way as a conventional car, but this is not what the 4x4 accessory culture is all about. 4x4s are accessorized with items such as bull bars, side steps, roof access ladders, extra driving lights and spare-wheel covers with special graphics; some are even equipped with bodykits and others are subjected to major work such as an engine transplant.

There are two points to remember about such vehicles when examining them with a view to purchase. First: do not be persuaded to pay extra for a vehicle which has accessories you do not want and will probably remove as soon as you get a chance. Remember, for example, that side steps will compromise a vehicle's off-road ability, and that there is currently a debate over whether bull bars cause avoidable injury to pedestrians struck by 4x4s and should therefore be outlawed for road use. Second: make an extra check to ensure that any item which is not part of the vehicle's original specification has been properly fitted. It is not uncommon for extra lights to be wired in a positively dangerous fashion or for engine transplants to be accompanied by some crude metal surgery.

The lightweight 4x4 in context

Over the years, the 4x4 market has gone through a number of different trends which have affected the design of the vehicles themselves. Before the mid-Forties, almost all off-road vehicles were designed for military use. In fact the Willys Jeep which inspired so many later lightweight 4x4 designs was drawn up purely for military use during the Second World War.

The 4x4s which followed it in the Forties and Fifties were all utility vehicles, even though some of them were also capable of carrying passengers. The Sixties saw the first deviations from this norm as American-built vehicles like the International Scout of 1961, the Ford Bronco of 1965 and the Chevrolet Blazer of 1967 added a recreational or 'fun' element. Yet all these vehicles retained the principles of the utility vehicle with its beam axles and rugged, leaf-spring suspension. In all cases, selectable four-wheel drive was employed, designers reasoning that running in two-wheel drive mode on the road minimized noise, fuel consumption and drivetrain wear. Some of these American vehicles added more powerful engines to the traditional utility cocktail in order to give a road performance which was more acceptable for everyday use.

The next stage in 4x4 development came with the 1970 Range Rover, which employed beam axles with long-travel coil spring suspension to give a more comfortable ride and permanent four-wheel drive to improve traction and handling on the road. Its powerful engine followed the tradition of American recreational 4x4s of the Sixties (and, ironically, was actually based on a

Sixties' American design). As the Seventies progressed, so Range Rover customers demanded more luxury and convenience features, and the concept of the luxury four-wheel drive estate for everyday use came into being.

The Eighties saw the first real explosion of the 4x4 market. Mercedes-Benz in Germany had anticipated this with the release of their G-Wagen in 1979, but the real innovators of the early Eighties were Japanese manufacturers. Following the Range Rover's success, they had identified a customer group which wanted the British vehicle's roadability and comfort levels at a cheaper price, and was prepared to sacrifice some of the Range Rover's ultimate ability to get it. So the early Eighties saw the arrival of new and hugely influential 4x4s from Mitsubishi (the Shogun) and Isuzu (the Trooper). Other Japanese manufacturers, notably Toyota and Nissan, adapted existing rugged four-wheel drive estates to fill niches in this expanding market sector.

However, vehicles like these were essentially designed as family transport, and most of them were far too expensive to suit many younger buyers who had been attracted by the rugged image associated with four-wheel drives. The vehicles which came to cater for their interests in the early Eighties were adaptations of smaller 4x4s which had originally been designed as rough-terrain runabouts for countries without roads. They were the Russian Lada Niva and the Japanese Suzuki SJ, the latter of which had been drawn up for markets in South-East Asia. The Suzuki, better-built and more easily adapted to the demands of a fashion-conscious market, was an enormous success and established a new market for short-wheelbase recreational vehicles.

As 4x4 vehicles began to reach an increasingly wide cross-section of buyers towards the end of the Eighties, so a new factor entered the equation. Buyers switching from saloon cars soon noticed that even the best of the 4x4s did not enjoy the same ease of driving as the cars they were used to, and demand soon arose for better handling, better performance and less of the utility-vehicle *ambience* which was a hangover from the Sixties and earlier. So it was that the Nineties saw manufacturers designing 4x4s which were increasingly more car-like in their road behaviour. The pioneer was Suzuki, whose 1989 Vitara was a remarkable worldwide success and precisely captured the mood of the market; several others followed.

It had, of course, been clear for some considerable time that those who bought 4x4s for the image they conveyed hardly ever used them in the demanding off-road conditions they were built to tackle. The independent front suspensions characteristic of Eighties' Japanese vehicles could prove a liability in some off-road conditions, but that had not been a deterrent to the buyers. The logical next step was to build a 4x4 which looked the part but which dispensed with the expensive hardware of the traditional off-roader and was biased towards everyday road use. It was Toyota who achieved this, with 1994's RAV-4, which had monocoque construction (instead of a separate chassis and body), all-independent suspension (instead of beam axles), a high-performance engine and no transfer box to provide crawler gears for off-road work. It will no doubt be followed by others which take the basic concept further.

ASIA ROCSTA

Background

'Asia' is a relatively new name in the European 4x4 market, although the South Korean company behind it has been building light four-wheel drives for many years, not least for the South Korean military. Since 1976, Asia Motors (of Seoul) has actually belonged to Kia Motors, and both companies have enjoyed links with the Japanese Mazda concern.

It was Mazda which designed the Rocsta's 1.8-litre petrol engine, a power-plant available in the 626 saloon until 1992. It was Mazda, too, which was responsible for the 2.2-litre diesel alternative. However, these powerplants were perhaps the newest elements of the vehicle. It is, in fact, a civilian derivative of the Korean Army's standard ¼-ton light utility, itself derived from the Jeep CJ-5 which was last built in 1983.

Nevertheless, Asia Motors turned the age of the basic design to good advantage. Its appearance appealed to the fashion for 'retro' styling which also underpinned the success of Mahindra's Jeep-derived models and to some extent of the Jeep Wrangler itself. A few gaudy side-stripes made their contribution to the vehicle's fashionable appeal, and the economical four-cylinder engines provided adequate performance without the fuel-guzzling tendencies of the big sixes and V8s associated with authentic Jeeps. However, the least said about the Rocsta name (try reading it as 'rock star') the better; no doubt it sounds enormously chic in non-English-speaking countries, but it tends to make British buyers cringe.

The Asia Rocsta entered production during 1990, but was not announced for the British market until 1993, examples not becoming available through the showrooms until early the following year. The first 12 months of sales saw fewer than 600 examples sold, so this is not a common 4x4 in Britain. Nevertheless, it does appeal to a niche market. The Rocsta can be bought in either hardtop or soft-top configuration, and there is also a van derivative of the hardtop for the commercial market.

Korea's Rocsta is a civilian derivative of the country's military utility vehicle, which in turn was inspired by the American Jeep.

13

Vital statistics

Engine:	1,789cc petrol four-cylinder, with 77bhp at 5,500rpm and 98lb.ft at 3,000rpm or 2,184cc diesel four-cylinder, with 61bhp at 4,050rpm and 93lb.ft at 2,500rpm	
Transmission:	Five-speed manual Selectable four-wheel drive Freewheeling front hubs (manually engaged)	
Suspension:	Live front and rear axles; leaf springs all round; anti-roll bar on the front axle	
Steering:	Unassisted	
Brakes:	Ventilated front discs and rear drums with power assistance as standard	
Dimensions:	Wheelbase	83.9in (2,132mm)
	Length	140.9in (3,581mm)
	Height	73in (1,854mm)
	Width	65.9in (1,676mm)
	Ground clearance	8.1in (205mm)
	Weight Petrol models	3,681lb (1,670kg)
	Diesel models	3,748lb (1,700kg)
Number of seats:	4	
Towing capacity:	2,200lb (1,000kg)	
Insurance rating:	Group 7	
Fuel consumption:	Petrol models	24.5mpg
	Diesel models	23.2mpg
Top speed:	Petrol models	80mph
	Diesel models	70mph
0–60mph:	Petrol models	20.2sec
	Diesel models	23sec

Character summary

The Rocsta has a quite distinctive character as an 'image' vehicle for younger buyers. Some of its elements – the side-stripes, the fake windscreen hinges – are purely designed for the sake of appearances yet equipment levels are quite basic in order to keep the showroom price down. Similarly, the vehicle's compact dimensions make it only just big enough for four people, and with four up there is very little luggage space available behind the seats.

Strictly speaking, this is a 4x4 for young singles and young couples who do not need much carrying space and are more concerned with image than practicality. This category of buyer is forgiving about the length of time necessary to erect the complicated soft-top; buyers with families would soon find such design weaknesses an irritation.

Nevertheless, build quality overall is good, and the GRP hardtop fits well.

Lockable cubbies under the front seats are a sensible if rather awkward solution to the problem of secure storage in a vulnerable open vehicle. Various optional items such as bull bars, side steps, spare-wheel covers and even wood trim can be purchased to personalize the Rocsta's appearance.

The Asia Rocsta is available in both hardtop and soft-top forms and with a choice of Mazda petrol or diesel engines.

Performance summary

The Rocsta is rather like a traditional Jeep or an early Land Rover to drive: it is noisy and draughty, with a ride which only young people will tolerate for long periods. However, the controls feel much more modern, with a light clutch and a gearchange which is smooth if a little sloppy. The petrol engine is the one to go for if the vehicle is going to be used mainly on the road. The diesel has better low-down torque for off-road use; on the road, however, despite a fair degree of refinement and a reasonably responsive nature, it offers less performance than the petrol alternative for no improvement in fuel economy.

The unassisted steering feels vague and has little self-centering action, and the turning circle is large for a vehicle of this size. There is plenty of understeer in corners, and the back end can be unsettled on bumpy bends. Even on dead straight roads, the Rocsta's leaf-spring suspension promotes plenty of pitch and wallow. Worth knowing is that very early vehicles had eight-leaf springs which gave a very rough ride indeed; the importers quickly changed these for four-leaf springs with an additional helper leaf, and these did improve the ride considerably.

Off the road, the short wheelbase and short overhangs both front and rear allow the Rocsta to give quite a good account of itself. However, axle travel is limited (as with most leaf-sprung vehicles) and the heavily-damped steering can make it difficult for the driver to determine what the front wheels are doing. The plastic mouldings along the lower edges of the body are also vulnerable to damage.

Reliability, weaknesses, spares

The Rocsta has not been available in Britain for long enough to make a balanced judgment about its reliability. However, initial indications are good, and there appear to be no major problems with spare parts availability.

Key specification changes in the UK

1993 (Oct):   Announced at motor show
1994 (Mar):   First showroom deliveries

Nomenclature

DX   High-line specification, with cloth seat facings (instead of vinyl), alloy wheels and adjustable steering column

Resale values

It is too early yet to assess resale values accurately. Nevertheless, early indications are favourable.

Further reading

All models: *Off Road and 4 Wheel Drive*, December 1993
Off Road and 4 Wheel Drive, October 1994
Diesel: *International Off-Roader*, November 1994

DACIA DUSTER

Background

The Dacia Duster dates from the bad old days when Romania was part of the Communist Bloc and all motor manufacturers were owned by the state. It was the result of collaboration between ARO (who had built Soviet GAZ 4x4s under licence in Romania since 1964) and Dacia (who had close links with Renault and had been building some of the French company's products under licence since 1966).

The collaboration between the two produced a recreational 4x4 which made its debut in 1979 under the title of the ARO 10-series and used Dacia-built Renault engines. Sold in other European countries as AROs, these came to Britain as Dacia Dusters in 1985. The Dacia name was chosen because Britain was already familiar with the Dacia Denem, a licence-built Renault 12 introduced in 1982.

The history of the Duster in Britain has been plagued by problems with the importers. Plans announced to bring the vehicles in during 1982 were held up when the first importers ceased trading; there was a hiccup in autumn 1990 when the new importers gave way to a third company; and then imports ceased in 1993, apparently permanently. The last Duster was sold in Britain in September 1993, but the vehicle remains available in Romania and in other European countries, as the ARO 10-series.

As a result, the Duster does not enjoy a good reputation in Britain. Fundamentally, however, it is a soundly-conceived lightweight 4x4 aimed at the cheap end of the recreational market.

The diesel-engined version of the Romanian-built and Renault-powered Dacia Duster, last imported into the UK in 1993.

Vital statistics

Engine:	1,397cc carburettor petrol four-cylinder, with 65bhp at 5,250rpm and 77lb.ft at 3,000rpm or 1,596cc indirect-injection diesel four-cylinder, with 57bhp at 4,800rpm and 74lb.ft at 2,500rpm (1989–1993)
Transmission:	Four-speed manual Selectable four-wheel drive Freewheeling front hubs (manually engaged)
Suspension:	Independent front suspension with wishbones and coil springs; live rear axle with semi-elliptic leaf springs
Steering:	Unassisted
Brakes:	Discs on the front wheels and drums at the rear, with power assistance as standard

Dimensions:

Wheelbase	94.5in (2,400mm)
Length	148.7in (3,777mm)
Height	68.5in (1,740mm)
Width	63in (1,600mm)
Ground clearance	8.5in (225mm)
Weight	GL, GLX and Roadster Plus 2,645lb (1,200kg) GLD 2,910lb (1,320kg)

Number of seats:	5
Towing capacity:	3,195lb (1,450kg)
Insurance rating:	Group 4 (petrol) Group 5 (diesel)
Fuel consumption:	Petrol models 25mpg Diesel models 28mpg
Top speed:	Petrol models 76mph Diesel models 70mph
0–60mph:	Petrol models 23.5sec Diesel models 25.7sec

Character summary

The square-rigged Duster somehow contrives to look too flimsy to be a credible 4x4, especially in soft-top Roadster guise. Always intended as a cheap vehicle to buy, its general aura is exactly that. As an inexpensive recreational vehicle, it has some interest as a secondhand buy. However, its general lack of credibility in off-roading circles means that it is not perhaps the most sensible buy for weekend fun in the mud. Similarly, the Duster's negative image may be sufficient reason for not buying one as an everyday vehicle.

The interior is drab, plasticky and not at all inviting. However, in purely

The lack of a current dealer network places the Duster firmly at the cheaper end of the recreational vehicle market. This Roadster Plus model, with white hood and black trim, was introduced in 1989.

practical terms, the Duster is a reasonably spacious short-wheelbase four-seater. The five people it should carry in theory will not find it very comfortable. Luggage-space is also limited when all the seats are in use.

Performance summary

The Duster's road performance is adequate but rather lacklustre, especially in diesel-powered form. Handling and roadholding are also unremarkable, although more power under the bonnet would probably expose some weaknesses. The gearchange is heavy and awkward, and the steering rather wooden. Overall, this is not an inspiring vehicle to drive on the road.

Off the road, the Duster justifies itself rather better. The fairly short wheelbase and short overhangs allow it to perform quite well, although the small 14in wheels mean that ground clearance under the axles can often be less than with other lightweight 4x4s. Torque delivery is only adequate with either engine, but the Duster manages to clamber about well enough to be an enjoyable recreational vehicle.

Reliability, weaknesses, spares

The build quality of the Duster was always variable and often doubtful. Particular weaknesses include the soft-top. However, the mechanical components – many of Renault origin although made in Romania – are generally reliable.

As the Duster is no longer sold in Britain, spares will be problematical. However, many Renault components can be used to keep a vehicle in mechanical health. It is also worth remembering that the Duster is still sold in several continental European countries, and that spares should be available through ARO dealers there.

Key specification changes in the UK
1985 (Apr):   Duster GLX 3-door introduced, with 1.4-litre petrol engine
1986 (Sep):   One-piece tailgate and rear wash-wipe added; cloth seat facings replaced all-vinyl upholstery
1987 (Feb):   GL model introduced
1988 (Dec):   Roadster Plus introduced
1989 (Oct):   Twin headlamps and new grille; rev counter added
1989 (Dec):   GLD diesel Estate introduced
1990 (Feb):   GLX Showman introduced
1990 (Aug):   GL petrol models no longer imported
1993 (Sep):   Duster no longer imported

Nomenclature
GL   1987–1993 Basic trim
GLD   1989–1993 Diesel Estate
GLX   1984–1993 Estate with high-line trim
Roadster Plus   1989 Soft-top model with white hood and black trim
Showman   1990 Limited-edition version of GLX, with bull bar, colour-coded alloy wheels and spare-wheel cover; limited edition brass plate inside

Resale values
Now that the Duster is no longer imported to the UK or supported by a dealer network, resale values have sunk through the floor. As a result, very few Dusters will be sold through trade outlets; most will change hands privately.

Further reading
All models: *Off Road and 4 Wheel Drive*, May 1985
Roadster: *Off Road and 4 Wheel Drive*, November 1985

DAIHATSU FOURTRAK

Background

The original Daihatsu Fourtrak was introduced to Britain three years after its 1974 launch in Japan, but made very little impact on the market. Known to its makers as the F10 Taft, it was sold primarily as a commercial vehicle in Britain.

However, the second-generation Fourtrak (known as a Daihatsu Rocky in many markets outside Britain) made much more of an impact after it was introduced in June 1984. For a start, it was a far better and more versatile vehicle than the rather diminutive original; and by 1984 the boom in four-wheel drive estates had begun. Nevertheless, the British importers did not lose sight of the commercial market, and the Fourtrak was also made available in van and long-wheelbase pick-up forms.

As a passenger-carrier, the Fourtrak was available in two wheelbase lengths. The longer of these proved the more popular, carrying the Estate body with its kicked-up rear roofline to provide headroom in the back. The short-wheelbase chassis was used for the Sport models (as well as for the van variants), which always had a flat roofline and were eventually dropped in favour of the Sportrak. Both petrol and diesel derivatives were available, but the most popular was the 2.8-litre turbodiesel, an excellent engine which made the Fourtrak Estate into a viable alternative to a conventional family estate car.

The Fourtrak always had a traditional ladder-frame chassis, beam axles with leaf springs and an all-steel body. It was replaced in 1993 by the Fourtrak Independent, which was essentially the same vehicle fitted with wider-track axles and independent front suspension.

The Daihatsu Fourtrak EL turbodiesel, a high-line model in the estate range.

Vital statistics

Engine: 1,998cc four-cylinder petrol, with 87bhp at
4,600rpm and 116lb.ft at 3,000rpm
(1984–1988)
or 2,237cc four-cylinder petrol, with 90bhp at
4,200rpm and 132lb.ft at 2,500rpm
(1992–1993)
or 2,765cc four-cylinder diesel, with 72bhp at
3,600rpm and 125lb.ft at 2,200rpm
(1984–1991, and later commercials)
or 2,765cc four-cylinder turbodiesel, with
87bhp at 3,600rpm and 155lb.ft at 2,200rpm
(1990–1993)
or 2,765cc four-cylinder intercooled
turbodiesel, with 100bhp at 3,400rpm and
181lb.ft at 1,900rpm (1991 on)

Transmission: Five-speed manual
Selectable four-wheel drive
Automatic freewheeling front hubs

Suspension: Live front axle with semi-elliptic leaf springs and
anti-roll bar; live rear axle with semi-elliptic leaf
springs and three-stage electrically adjustable
dampers on LWB models (1984–1993)

Steering: Power-assisted as standard

Brakes: Ventilated discs at the front and drums at the
rear, with power assistance as standard

Dimensions:

Wheelbase	SWB	87in (2,210mm)
	LWB	99.6in (2,530mm)
Length	SWB	150in (3,810mm)
	LWB	163in (4,140mm)
Height	SWB	72in (1,829mm)
	LWB	75.4in (1,915mm)
Width	1984–1993	62in (1,574mm)
	1993 on	70.5in (1,791mm)
Ground clearance		8.3in (210mm)
Weight		SWB 2-litre petrol 3,042lb (1,380kg)
		SWB 2.2-litre petrol 3,252lb (1,475kg)
		LWB Turbodiesel 3,285lb (1,490kg)

Number of seats:	SWB	4/5
	LWB	7
Towing capacity:	SWB	6,400lb (2,900kg)
	LWB	7,715lb (3,500kg)
Insurance rating:	Group 8	
Fuel consumption:	1,998cc petrol models 18–28mpg	
	2,237cc petrol models 17–25mpg	
	Turbodiesel models 25–35mpg	
Top speed:	1,998cc petrol models 81mph	
	2,237cc petrol models 85mph	
	Turbodiesel models 84mph	
	Intercooled turbodiesel models 85mph	
0–60mph:	1,998cc petrol models 17.9sec	
	2,237cc petrol models 17.5sec	
	Turbodiesel models 18sec	
	Intercooled turbodiesel models 16sec	

Character summary

The long-wheelbase Fourtrak Estate has always been viewed as a very good family vehicle, with plenty of interior space despite its relatively compact dimensions and the tall and narrow cabin. However, it actually feels rather more spacious than it is, thanks to clever design and the large glass area. Five people and their luggage can be accommodated in reasonable comfort, but the Fourtrak Estate only takes a full complement of seven passengers if the two sitting in the rearmost seats are children. On space, the vehicle simply cannot compete with big off-roaders like the Mitsubishi Shogun or Toyota Land Cruiser. With only three doors, access to the rear seats of the Fourtrak can also be awkward for the elderly or infirm and less than ideal for very small children.

The Fourtrak has an excellent reputation as a tow vehicle, especially in turbodiesel Estate form. It is easy to live with as an everyday 4x4 and feels well built and sturdy. The angular styling and strictly functional facia – neither is very imaginative – both contribute to this impression.

The early Sport models on the short wheelbase are rather less versatile than the Estate models. They offer less interior space and are a little too utilitarian to appeal to the recreational 4x4 market. Daihatsu recognized this and replaced them with the Sportrak, which was designed specifically for that market.

A Fourtrak Estate represents a good combination of family hack and weekend fun machine for buyers who have to combine the two in one vehicle.

Performance summary

One reason for the Fourtrak's success was that it offered no surprises to the driver used to a conventional car, and that remains the case today. Accelera-

The Fourtrak TDX estate, powered by a 2.8-litre four-cylinder intercooled turbodiesel, a versatile vehicle with a good towing reputation.

tion is more sluggish, of course, and the ride considerably rougher with the semi-elliptic leaf spring suspension, but roadholding is good and the handling nicely neutral. Worth knowing is that early models had stiffer road springs and give a harsher ride than later examples. The adjustable dampers on Estate models are also more of a gimmick than a real benefit.

Noise can be intrusive, with wind roar from the windscreen pillars on all models at speed and engine noise from the turbodiesel and 2.2-litre petrol variants. The post-1987 diesels with their belt-driven camshafts did improve on noise levels over the earlier types, but diesel drone is still present at cruising speeds.

Both intercooled and non-intercooled versions of the turbodiesel engine give good low and mid-range acceleration. In fact, performance with the turbodiesels is in most respects better than with the petrol engines. The gearbox is slick, although it can be rather notchy when cold.

Off the road, the Fourtrak performs very well indeed for a leaf-sprung vehicle, and here the short-wheelbase Sport models do rather better than the long-wheelbase Estates. However, the stiff springs can make the ride rather bouncy, and they also limit the axle travel.

Reliability, weaknesses, spares
The basic engineering of the Fourtrak is simple, which is no doubt one reason why very little seems to go wrong with the vehicle. Despite the all-steel construction, rust is not a problem. Fourtraks were sold with an eight-year warranty against rust when new, which indicates that Daihatsu had a lot of faith in their galvanized body panels and in the effectiveness of their annual anti-rust inspection.

The most vulnerable area is the interior: after high mileages, the vinyl side panels on the seats tend to split, and the dashboard starts to creak and rattle. Post-1991 models also had lights mounted in the bumper instead of at waist height in the bodywork, and these are quite easily damaged. Daihatsu dealers offer a conversion kit to enable a second set of lights to be fitted in the original positions at waist height.

Everyday spares can sometimes be surprisingly costly, but everything is readily available from a well-organized chain of Daihatsu dealers in the UK.

Key specification changes in the UK

1984 (Jun):   SWB range introduced to UK with petrol and diesel engines, as hardtops or soft-tops

1985 (Oct):   LWB EL Estate and Fourtrak Sport introduced, both with petrol or diesel engine

1987 (Jun):   Limited Edition of 210 turbodiesel Estates, based on EL, with Gunmetal and Silver paintwork

1987 (Oct):   Limited Edition EL turbodiesel with all-black paintwork

1987 (Dec):   Softer suspension; belt-driven camshaft replaced gear-drive in diesel engines; new seats with side bolsters and head restraints; square headlamps replaced circular type

1988 (Feb):   Soft-top and Sport models discontinued. EX turbodiesel model introduced

1988 (Dec):   Petrol models deleted

The limited-edition Fourtrak 2.8 TDX SE, which was first supplied in August 1991 and presented in a metallic green paint finish.

25

1990 (Jan):	EL upgraded with central locking, electric front windows and improved front seat adjustment; turbodiesel available on basic models
1990 (Aug):	Limited Edition of 200 turbodiesel Estates, based on EL, with Black and Grey paintwork
1991 (Apr):	Revised range with new model names: new grilles and modified suspension; rear lamp clusters relocated in bumper; intercooler added to turbodiesel engines
1991 (Aug):	Limited Edition TDX 2.8 SE, based on TDX, with metallic green paintwork
1992 (Feb):	2.2-litre petrol engine introduced
1992 (Jun):	Further quantities of TDX 2.8 SE available
1993 (Oct):	Range replaced by Fourtrak Independent

Nomenclature

DL	1991–1993, basic turbodiesel Estate
DS	1991–1993, SWB with naturally aspirated diesel
DX	1985–1991, basic turbodiesel Estate
EL	1985–1991, high-line Estate
ELT	1985–1991, turbodiesel
EX	1988–1991, high-line turbodiesel Estate
EXT	1984–1985, turbodiesel
GX	1991–1993, Estate
Sport	1985–1988, SWB petrol or diesel, hardtop or soft-top with special wheels and other equipment
TDL	1991–1993, high-line intercooled turbodiesel Estate
TDS	1991–1993, basic turbodiesel Estate
TDX	1991–1993, intercooled turbodiesel Estate; also TDX 2.8 SE Limited Editions

Resale values

Fourtraks do keep their value well, although the availability of the newer Fourtrak Independent and sheer age means that values of the earliest models have begun to drop more sharply. Generally speaking, however, there is a simple rule of thumb to follow: turbodiesels keep their value better than petrol models and Estates keep their value better than Sports.

Further reading

All models:	*International Off-Roader*, June 1993
	Off Road and 4 Wheel Drive, November 1993
EL turbodiesel:	*Autocar and Motor*, November 18, 1987
	Diesel Car, July 1989
EX turbodiesel:	*Off Road and 4 Wheel Drive*, July 1985
GX 2.2 petrol:	*International Off-Roader*, March 1993
TDX turbodiesel:	*International Off-Roader*, March 1993
	Diesel Car, August 1991

DAIHATSU FOURTRAK INDEPENDENT

Background

The Daihatsu Fourtrak Independent replaced the established and popular Fourtrak from the same company during 1993. However, the new vehicle was really a re-engineered version of the old, incorporating independent front suspension and coil springs at the rear (to improve the ride quality) and wider tracks (to improve the handling) as the primary changes. The new features were also carried over onto the commercial models, which now went under the name of Fourtrak Fieldman.

The basic line-up was not changed from that of the previous and successful Fourtrak range. That meant that there was a short-wheelbase model which shared its flat-roof bodyshell with the Fieldman vans and a long-wheelbase Estate model with a raised rear roofline to cater for the family market. Nevertheless, the Fourtrak Independent range did not include any petrol-engined variants; Daihatsu had instead standardized on the 2.8-litre intercooled turbodiesel (with the old naturally-aspirated diesel engine also available on Fieldman commercial models).

One omission from the range was an automatic-transmission model. This was an area which Daihatsu had not tackled with the previous Fourtrak range either, but it undoubtedly cost them sales in an era when the family-estate market was increasingly turning to turbodiesel models with automatic transmission.

The Fourtrak Independent has sold well, but has not emulated the success of its predecessor models in the UK. One reason is the increased number of competitive vehicles from other manufacturers; another must surely be the age of the basic design.

Vital statistics

Engine:	2,765cc four-cylinder intercooled turbodiesel, with 100bhp at 3,400rpm and 181lb.ft at 1,900rpm
Transmission:	Five-speed manual Selectable four-wheel drive Automatic freewheeling front hubs
Suspension:	Independent front suspension with twin wishbones and torsion bars; live rear axle with coil springs
Steering:	Power-assisted as standard
Brakes:	Ventilated discs at the front and drums at the rear, with power assistance as standard

Dimensions:	Wheelbase	99.6in (2,530mm)
	Length	164in (4,165mm)
	Height	75.4in (1,915mm)
	Width	67in (1,702mm)
	Ground clearance	8.3in (210mm)
	Weight	SWB 3,663lb (1,661kg)
		LWB 3,839lb (1,741kg)
Number of seats:	SWB 5	
	LWB 7	
Towing capacity:	7,717lb (3,500kg)	
Insurance rating:	Group 8	
Fuel consumption:	25–35mpg	
Top speed:	85mph	
0–60mph:	16sec	

Independent front suspension, coil springs at the rear and wider front and rear tracks distinguish the Independent from its predecessor.

The Independent 2.8 TDS, the short-wheelbase version of the Fourtrak introduced into the UK at the end of 1993.

Character summary

Most of the comments already made about the earlier Fourtrak also apply to the Fourtrak Independent. The tall and narrow cabin was not improved in the facelift, but the intelligent interior design makes the best use of the space available, and the large glass area prevents any feelings of claustrophobia for the occupants.

However, the Fourtrak Independent has so far failed to shake off the rather utilitarian image associated with the older model. One reason is that it looks so similar; another is that it has acquired no additional soundproofing to bring noise levels down to those of newer competitive vehicles. While the Independent is actually a much more civilized vehicle than the older Fourtrak in many respects, it does not aspire to the chic appeal of family 4x4s like the Land Rover Discovery or Vauxhall Frontera. As a dual-purpose vehicle, alternating between workhorse and family transport, it nevertheless works well. The strong pulling power of the standard intercooled turbodiesel engine and the extra stability brought by the widened tracks make it an even better tow vehicle than before.

Performance summary

The Fourtrak Independent is a much more competent performer on the road than its leaf-sprung predecessors. The main difference is in the ride, which has lost all trace of harshness and is now comfortable and compliant. However, there is often a trade-off in terms of handling when a vehicle's suspension is made softer, and so it proves with the Fourtrak Independent. The independent front suspension and coil-sprung rear end allow much more body-roll in corners than the hard leaf springs of the older models. The wider tracks prevent this from developing into a problem, but the additional roll certainly is noticeable from inside the vehicle.

Otherwise, the Fourtrak Independent has all the best features of the final old-model Fourtraks, including the gutsy and fuel-efficient intercooled turbo-diesel engine. On TDX models, push-button selection of four-wheel drive on the move is a useful additional feature.

Reliability, weaknesses, spares

The Fourtrak Independent has proved to be more reliable in service than its predecessors. It has no particular weaknesses and spares are readily available through Daihatsu dealers. Some spares can be expensive – one result of dealers selling so few because the vehicles are fundamentally reliable.

Key specification changes in the UK

1993 (Oct):   Fourtrak Independent range introduced in LWB form, with independent front suspension, coil-sprung rear axle, widened tracks, wide wheelarches and revised interior
1993 (Nov):   SWB Fourtrak Independent introduced
1995 (Jan):   Timberline special editions available on both wheelbases

Nomenclature

TDS   SWB models
TDL   Basic LWB models
TDX   High-line LWB models
Timberline 1995 special editions, with paintwork in Green and Grey and side graphics

Resale values

The Fourtrak Independent models have upheld the Daihatsu tradition for strong resale values in the two years since they were introduced to the UK. There is no discernible difference in depreciation between short-wheelbase and long-wheelbase models.

Further reading

TDS *Off Road and 4 Wheel Drive*, April 1994
     International Off-Roader, August 1994
TDX *Diesel Car*, November 1993
     International Off-Roader, April 1994

DAIHATSU SPORTRAK

Background

Although the Sportrak shares many styling cues with the established Fourtrak range, it is actually a very different vehicle with a much shorter wheelbase and no diesel engine option: all Sportraks have been powered by a high-revving petrol engine which first saw service in Daihatsu saloon cars.

The Sportrak was Daihatsu's entry into the recreational and image 4x4 market. It was announced towards the end of 1988 and became available early the following year. From the beginning, it was intended as a chic urban runabout with the ability to go off-road occasionally. However, it was bested by the Suzuki Vitara, which offered much more radical styling and looked less like a traditional 4x4. Despite what is probably a better off-road performance than the Vitara, the Sportrak has never had quite the same appeal – which says a lot about the real reasons behind many young buyers' choice of a 4x4. From 1994, a cheaper base model was introduced to improve sales, and a year later an even cheaper entry-level Sportrak Xi was announced.

Nevertheless, the Sportrak – a Daihatsu Feroza in Japan and most other markets – did lead the field by being the first 4x4 vehicle ever to have a multi-valve engine (the 1.6-litre petrol engine has four valves per cylinder to give 16 valves in all). It also became the first vehicle to follow the lead set by the Toyota RAV-4, and in Italy and Switzerland its 1995 Feroza Full-time version featured permanent four-wheel drive without a transfer box to give reduction gearing for off-road use.

The Sportrak has always had a single basic body style with a rollover bar behind the front seats and a removable cab roof. To this can be added either hard or soft-tops, although the hardtop version has always been more popular in the UK, where soft-tops tend to lose their appeal in the winter months.

Vital statistics

Engine:	1,598cc four-cylinder carburettor petrol, with 85bhp at 6,000rpm and 93lb.ft at 3,500rpm (to 1990) 1,598cc four-cylinder injected petrol, with 94bhp at 5,700rpm and 95lb.ft at 4,800rpm (1990 on)
Transmission:	Five-speed manual Selectable four-wheel drive Freewheeling front hubs with manual locks (to March 1991) or automatic locks (from March 1991, except EXi)
Suspension:	Independent front suspension with wishbones, torsion bar springs and anti-roll bar

	Live rear axle with semi-elliptic leaf springs; three-stage adjustable dampers on all models except EXi	
Steering:	Power-assisted as standard (from March 1991)	
Brakes:	Discs at the front and drums at the rear Power assistance standard	
Dimensions:	Wheelbase	85.6in (2,175mm)
	Length	1988–1991: 145in (3,685mm) 1991 on: 149in (3,785mm)
	Height	67.9in (1,725mm)
	Width	1988–1991: 62.2in (1,580mm) 1991 on: 64.4in (1,635mm)
	Ground clearance	8.1in (205mm)
	Weight	1988–1991: 2,436lb (1,105kg) 1991 on: 2,788lb (1,265kg)
Number of seats:	4	
Towing capacity:	3,306lb (1,500kg)	
Insurance rating:	Group 10 (DX and EL) Group 11 (EFi) Group 12 (STi, ELi and ELXi)	
Fuel consumption:	26–31mpg	
Top speed:	95mph	
0–60mph:	11.7sec	

Character summary

The Sportrak was designed as a chic urban 4x4 for young singles or couples without families, everything about it reflecting those design priorities. It is compact, comes only as a three-door, and offers sparkling acceleration and the sort of handling more familiar to the owners of hot hatches. In essence, it is designed as a vehicle to have fun with. Most buyers are far more interested in its looks and the image it conveys than in whether or not it can actually be driven off the road.

The down side to all this is that it is not very good as a long-distance cruiser. The biggest problems are noise (the 16-valve engine can become very thrashy at high speeds) and poor seats (there is insufficient side or lumbar support, particularly for tall drivers). Similarly, load space in the rear is minimal if all the seats are occupied.

Above, an early Sportrak EL, and below, later open-top and closed versions of the vehicle in ELX trim, all three indicating the Sportrak's positioning in the recreational as well as the chic urban 4x4 market.

Performance summary

That the Sportrak appeals to hot hatch drivers new to 4x4s is one of its strengths, and Daihatsu scored a number of sales on the back of that appeal. The vehicle is lively and responsive on the road, accelerating very much faster than most larger family 4x4s. It also corners well with little of the disturbing lean so characteristic of its bigger brothers. The gearchange is positive and slick, with low gearing to mask the torque deficiency of the engine at low revs.

However, the ride is hard and unforgiving, the stiff springing (which counters body roll in corners) joining with the short wheelbase to give a ride which is at best uncomfortable. Otherwise good all-round visibility is marred by the spare wheel mounted on the rear door, which can make reversing difficult.

Off the road, the Sportrak performs much better than its paper specification suggests. The short wheelbase and minimal overhangs are a help, but the engine must be revved hard to deliver enough torque for hill-climbing. The lack of bottom-end torque also means that engine braking on steep descents does not inspire confidence.

Reliability, weaknesses, spares

The Sportrak follows the great tradition of all Japanese vehicles by delivering unfailing mechanical reliability. Daihatsu dealers are generally extremely helpful and efficient, but spares can sometimes be pricey because there is little demand for them.

Nevertheless, the Sportrak does have a few weaknesses. The early carburettor engines often suffer from acceleration flat spots, a problem which was never fully sorted by Daihatsu and can still give trouble today. The sealing rubbers around the removable hardtop are easily damaged, while the hardtop itself (made of a resin-like material) can crack and is very expensive to replace. The quality of the ride has never been one of the Sportrak's better features, but a particularly bouncy or soft ride may be the result of having the adjustable dampers on the wrong setting: the best thing to do is to set them on 'Medium' and then leave them alone.

A 1994 Sportrak 1.6 ELXi with revised grille and headlamps, softer suspension and upgraded trim including the option of leather.

Key specification changes in the UK

1988 (Oct):   Sportrak announced for the UK, in hard and soft-top forms
1990 (Feb):   Limited Edition of 200 all-black EL models
1990 (Jly):   Soft-top models deleted; remaining models fitted with fuel-injected engine and catalytic converter
1990 (Aug):   Limited Edition of 600 EFi models in Black, White or Gunmetal with pink side graphics
1991 (Mar):   New model range introduced, including new soft-top; all models fitted with injected engine, larger bumpers (with lamps in rear bumper), restyled grille, relocated spare wheel and automatic freewheeling hubs in place of manual type; PAS standardized
1992 (Feb):   Limited Edition of 250 SE models, based on ELXi, with dark green paintwork and chromed wheels
1994 (Feb):   Cheaper EXi model replaced ELi; new front lights and grille with 'flying D' logo; softer rear suspension; trim upgraded on all models; leather option on ELXi
1995 (Jan):   Timberline special edition with Green and Grey paintwork and side graphics
1995 (Mar):   Xi entry-level model introduced

Nomenclature

DX   1989–1990, soft-top with carburettor engine
EFi   1990–1991, hardtop with injected engine
EL   1989–1990, hardtop with carburettor engine
ELi   1991–1993, hardtop with injected engine
ELXi   1991 on, high-line hardtop with injected engine, wide low-profile tyres and wheelarch extensions, electric windows and central locking
EXi   1994 on, soft-top with injected engine
STi   1991–1993, soft-top with injected engine
Xi   1995 on, entry-level hardtop model, with no rear seat

Resale values

Even though the Sportrak has begun to look a little dated and the importers appear to be struggling to maintain sales, resale values remain firm at the time of writing. As a general rule, hardtops hold their value better than soft-tops, and in this market the better-equipped models are the most sought-after and therefore hold their value best of all.

Further reading

All models: *International Off-Roader*, April 1994
EL: *Autocar and Motor*, March 29, 1989
ELXi: *Off Road and 4 Wheel Drive*, November 1991
              International Off-Roader, January 1992
EXi: *International Off-Roader*, August 1994

FORD MAVERICK

Background

The American arm of the Ford company had a tradition of 4x4 building going back as far as 1965, but the European side of the company had never made such a vehicle before work began on the Maverick. Recognizing that American 4x4 buyers have very different tastes from their European counterparts, Ford wisely decided against adapting an American vehicle for their first foray into this new market. Instead, they chose to develop a completely new vehicle in tandem with the Japanese Nissan company. Both companies would have the right to market versions of the new vehicle, and the Maverick was announced in 1993, at the same time as its Nissan Terrano II counterpart.

The Maverick and Terrano II were developed side-by-side at Nissan's European Technology Centre in Cranfield, and both vehicles are assembled on the same Spanish production lines at Nissan's Motor Iberica plant in Barcelona. Although Ford undoubtedly had an input and the Brighton-based IDEA design studio had a hand in the exterior styling, the major influences on

---

Vital statistics

Engine:	2,389cc injected petrol four-cylinder, with 124bhp at 5,200rpm and 146lb.ft at 2,200rpm
	or 2,663cc indirect-injection turbodiesel four-cylinder, with 99bhp at 4,000rpm and 164lb.ft at 2,200rpm
Transmission:	Five-speed manual
	Selectable four-wheel drive
	Automatic freewheeling front hubs
	Limited-slip differential in rear axle
Suspension:	Independent front suspension, with twin wishbones and torsion bar springs; live rear axle with coil springs
Steering:	Power-assisted as standard on all models
Brakes:	Ventilated discs at the front and drums at the rear, with standard power assistance
Dimensions:	Wheelbase SWB 96.4in (2,450mm)
	LWB 104.3in (2,650mm)
	Length SWB 162in (4,115mm)
	LWB 181in (4,597mm)
	Height 71in (1,803mm)
	Width 68in (1,727mm)
	Ground clearance SWB 8.46in (215mm)

The off-road ability of a long-wheelbase Maverick being put to the test.

Ground clearance	LWB 8.3in (210mm)	
Weight	SWB petrol 3,568lb (1,618kg)	
	SWB diesel 3,811lb (1,728kg)	
	LWB petrol 3,855lb (1,748kg)	
	LWB diesel 4,075lb (1,848kg)	
Number of seats:	SWB 4/5	
	LWB 7	
Towing capacity:	6,172lb (2,800kg)	
Insurance rating:	Group 10	
Fuel consumption:	SWB petrol	17–27mpg
	SWB diesel	22–32mpg
	LWB petrol	16–26mpg
	LWB diesel	22–32mpg
Top speed:	SWB petrol	99mph
	SWB diesel	90mph
	LWB petrol	99mph
	LWB diesel	90mph
0–60mph:	SWB petrol	13sec
	SWB diesel	18.5sec
	LWB petrol	13.7sec
	LWB diesel	19.5sec

the design were Japanese: the independent front suspension with torsion-bar springs; the tall, narrow body and the kick-up below the rear windows. The engines, too, are Nissan units. The main differences between Maverick and Terrano II are in fact in the front bumper, the grille and badging – and in the provision of a Ford radio in the Maverick!

The aim behind the joint project was to create a credible 4x4 with car-like handling; in other words, Ford and Nissan were following the lead set by Daihatsu with the Fourtrak and Suzuki with the Vitara. However, their aim was to cater for the family market with a long-wheelbase model, as well as for younger buyers who wanted a stylish short-wheelbase three-door. As a result, the Maverick was made available in two wheelbase lengths. Both petrol and turbodiesel engines are available, and Ford avoids a clash with Nissan in the UK by offering variants of the Maverick with specification levels and prices which are different from those of the Terrano II.

Although the Maverick was initially expected to sell three times as many examples as the Terrano II in Britain, in practice sales have been relatively slow. The problem may well have been in educating the public to think of Ford as a maker of 4x4s, but for whatever reason, the Maverick has not so far been the big hit Ford might have expected.

The Maverick name has been used on Fords before, most notably in the Seventies when the American Ford Maverick was one of the company's smaller cars. The name was also revived in Australia, where the Ford Maverick is actually a rebadged Nissan Patrol GR.

The five-door Maverick in GLX trim; a different grille, bumper and badging distinguish it from the equivalent Nissan Terrano II model.

The short-wheelbase three-door Maverick in basic LX guise; both 2.6-litre petrol and 2.7-litre turbodiesel engines are available.

Character summary

The Maverick was designed to feel like a conventional car, and it does. However, what that means is that the whole vehicle feels flimsy by the standards of other 4x4s, and that it lacks some of the essential character of a traditional off-roader.

The short-wheelbase models are the most car-like, and everything about them makes the former hot hatch driver feel at home; the biggest difference is that they are considerably higher off the ground. Even the long-wheelbase models feel most unlike other 4x4s to drive.

Both headroom and legroom benefit from the tall body, and the interiors are generally spacious. However, the short-wheelbase models are best considered as four-seaters, because a third passenger squeezed into the back is unlikely to be comfortable on a long journey. Similarly, the occasional seats in the rear of the long-wheelbase models do not offer enough comfort and support to make these vehicles into viable seven-seaters over long distances. Interior storage space for oddments is good in all models, but short-wheelbase models suffer from the usual failing of insufficient space behind the rear seats.

Performance summary

The most impressive aspects of the Maverick's behaviour are perhaps its car-like handling and impressively low noise levels. However, there are quite important character differences between short-wheelbase and long-wheelbase models. While the larger vehicles feel quite stable at all times, the short-wheelbase models can feel rather twitchy in bends. Similarly, the good ride of the long-wheelbase models is not reflected in the bounciness of the short-wheelbase types.

All varieties of Maverick are easy to drive, with well-weighted steering and progressive brakes, a smooth gearchange and a light clutch. The petrol-engined models are lively, while the turbodiesel engine gives plenty of refined power for motorway cruising.

Off the road, the turbodiesel engine has a disappointing lack of bottom-end torque. However, in all other respects the Maverick gives a good account of itself and it is pleasing that Ford and Nissan did not compromise off-road performance for the sake of good road behaviour. Naturally, the short-wheelbase models perform better than their long-wheelbase counterparts in extreme off-road conditions.

Reliability, weaknesses, spares

It is impossible to make a considered judgment of the Maverick's reliability at the time of writing, when the vehicle has been available for less than two years. However, no serious weaknesses have so far shown up, and all varieties have proved themselves to have the reliability normally associated with the Ford name. Spares should not prove a problem through the widespread Ford dealership network.

Key specification changes in the UK
1993 (Jun):   All models introduced to UK

Nomenclature
GLX   High-line models
LX   Basic models

Resale values

So far, the Maverick seems to be holding its value quite well in the used car market. However, the majority of used examples are being sold through Ford dealerships and it is therefore too early to tell whether resale prices are being artificially inflated.

Further reading
All models: *International Off-Roader*, August 1993
SWB petrol: *Autocar and Motor*, July 21, 1993
               Off Road and 4 Wheel Drive, December 1993
SWB diesel: *Off Road and 4 Wheel Drive*, October 1993

ISUZU TROOPER
(first generation)

Background

Isuzu was the last major Japanese manufacturer to enter the 4x4 market in Britain, and aimed its Trooper at the market opened up by Mitsubishi with the Shogun. However, the first-generation Troopers were always cheaper than the equivalent Shoguns, their success being largely attributable to this shrewd market positioning and to the importers' careful choice of model mix and specification from the wide variety offered by the factory.

The major seller in Britain was always the long-wheelbase family estate, but the importers did bring in short-wheelbase vehicles to compete in the weekend-fun and chic categories, and there were also limited numbers of commercials on the short-wheelbase chassis. Most popular of all Troopers were the turbodiesel long-wheelbase models. Three different specification levels (standard, Duty and Citation) allowed customers to tailor the models more precisely to their needs and budgets.

When the Trooper arrived in Britain during 1987, it was already a six-year-old design, having been launched in Japan in 1981. For that reason, its styling dated relatively quickly, and the first-generation Troopers were available in Britain for only five years before giving way to new models bearing the same name. In those five years, however, the Trooper had established a formidable and enduring reputation in the 4x4 market.

The Trooper is much liked because it is practical, easy to drive and – in turbodiesel form at least – not unduly expensive to run. However, its rather plain appearance is now causing it to look undistinguished alongside more modern 4x4s.

The Isuzu Trooper in long-wheelbase form, a practical and roomy estate.

The three-door short-wheelbase Trooper, aimed at the weekend fun market.

Vital statistics

Engine:	2,254cc carburettor four-cylinder petrol, with 108bhp at 4,600rpm and 123lb.ft at 2,600rpm (1987–1988)
	or 2,559cc injected four-cylinder petrol, with 111bhp at 5,000rpm and 138lb.ft at 2,500rpm (1988 on)
	or 2,238cc direct-injection four-cylinder turbodiesel, with 74bhp at 4,000rpm and 114lb.ft at 2,500rpm (1987–1988)
	or 2,771cc direct-injection four-cylinder turbodiesel, with 95bhp at 3,800rpm and 153lb.ft at 2,100rpm (1988 on)
Transmission:	Five-speed manual
	Four-speed automatic option with petrol engines (1988 on)
	Selectable four-wheel drive
	Freewheeling front hubs, automatic on manual transmission models and manual on automatics
	Limited-slip rear differential on Duty and Citation models
Suspension:	Independent front suspension with double wishbones and torsion bar springs
	Live rear axle with semi-elliptic leaf springs
Steering:	Power-assisted as standard
Brakes:	Disc brakes at the front; drums at the rear (1987–1988) or discs at the rear (1988 on)

Character summary

The Trooper is a tough, practical and ultimately sensible 4x4. In short-wheelbase three-door form, it appeals as an everyday vehicle for those without families, and as one which will double as a source of weekend fun. In long-wheelbase five-door form, it is a commodious family estate with inoffensive if unimaginative styling. In Citation trim, its equipment levels verge on the luxurious.

Performance summary

All first-generation Troopers are easy to drive, with a car-like gearchange (or effective automatic box) and pleasantly-weighted power steering. Motorway cruising is quiet and relaxed in both short and long-wheelbase types. The leaf-sprung rear axle is the weakest link in the suspension, giving an adequate ride in long-wheelbase models but causing unladen short-wheelbase models to pitch and bounce.

Dimensions:	Wheelbase	SWB 90.6in (2,300mm)
		LWB 104.3in (2,650mm)
	Length	SWB 160.4in (4,075mm)
		LWB 172.4in (4,380mm)
	Height	70.9in (1,800mm)
	Width	60.5in (1,650mm)
	Weight	SWB 3,498–3,715lb
		(1,587–1,685kg)
		depending on model
		LWB 3,630–3,847lb
		(1,647–1,745kg)
		depending on model
Number of seats:	SWB 4	
	LWB 5/7	
Towing capacity:	6,063lb (2,750kg)	
Insurance rating:	Petrol and 2.2 turbodiesel: Group 9	
	2.8 turbodiesel: Group 10	
	All Citation models: Group 11	
Fuel consumption:	Petrol models:	13–23mpg
	Turbodiesel models:	23–33mpg
Top speed:	2.3-litre petrol models:	75mph
	2.6-litre petrol models:	93mph
	2.2-litre turbodiesels:	83mph
	2.8-litre turbodiesels:	87mph est.
0–60mph:	2.3-litre petrol models:	16sec est.
	2.6-litre petrol models:	14sec est.
	2.2-litre turbodiesels:	22sec est.
	2.8-litre turbodiesels:	18sec est.

The road performance of the Troopers was always a strength, although the very early 2.2-litre turbodiesel is rather disappointing by more recent standards. The 2.3-litre petrol engine is smooth and willing, but the later 2.6-litre is altogether more responsive and satisfying. Best of all is the 2.8-litre turbodiesel, which is an excellent engine for most purposes, even though it lacks the top-end power to take even a short-wheelbase Trooper beyond 90mph.

The Trooper's independent front suspension has insufficient travel for serious off-road work, although the vehicle is competent enough over rough terrain. The best type for off-road use is a short-wheelbase 2.6-litre petrol model, whereas the best road vehicle is the long-wheelbase 2.8-litre turbodiesel. There is unfortunately no ideal compromise in this range of models for the buyer who wants the best of both worlds!

Reliability, weaknesses, spares

The first-generation Troopers boast an excellent record of mechanical reliability. They also have very few weaknesses: look out for excessive wear on the front tyres, which can often be caused by the front track going out of adjustment; beware, too, of seized drum brakes on the rear of early models – usually the result of inadequate maintenance. Chassis, paintwork, panels and interior trim are all hard-wearing, and only abused or neglected examples should show problems in these areas.

Spares can be obtained only through Isuzu dealers, as there are no aftermarket suppliers in Britain. The Isuzu dealership network has a good reputation.

Key specification changes in the UK

1987 (Feb):	Range introduced to Britain; standard and Duty trim levels available
1988 (Jan):	2.6-litre petrol replaced 2.3-litre; 2.8-litre turbodiesel replaced 2.2-litre; Citation trim level available for LWB turbodiesel only
1988 (Oct):	Citation trim available on all models; two-tone finishes with Duty and Citation options
1989 (Feb):	Revised trim; central locking operable from both front doors; interior revisions
1992 (Feb):	Replaced by second-generation Trooper range

Nomenclature

Citation	Top specification option, with limited-slip differential in the rear axle, air conditioning, electric windows, headlamp washers, cruise control, etc (slight variations from year to year)
Duty	Intermediate specification, with electric windows, headlamp washers, rear mudflaps and a limited-slip differential in the rear axle (slight variations from year to year)

A 1990 example of the long-wheelbase Trooper Citation, the vehicle with the most luxurious of the three trim and equipment levels offered with this range. Air conditioning, electric windows and headlamp washers are included in the standard package for this model.

Resale values

Long-wheelbase Troopers hold their value well, especially the 2.8-litre turbo-diesel models. Short-wheelbase models are very much less in demand and may prove harder to sell on. In the long term, the disappearance of the Trooper from the British market (as Vauxhall takes over with the Monterey) will probably cause damage to the Trooper's image and a consequent sharp fall in resale values.

Further reading

All models:	*Off Road and 4 Wheel Drive*, August 1992
	Off Road and 4 Wheel Drive, July 1993
	International Off-Roader, August 1993
SWB Citation turbodiesel:	*Diesel Car*, November 1990
LWB Citation turbodiesel:	*Diesel Car*, December 1988

ISUZU TROOPER
(second generation)

Background

Great things were expected of the second-generation Trooper, and in most respects Isuzu's effort did not disappoint. The new models which reached the UK in 1992 were undoubtedly faster, more refined and luxurious than their predecessors. However, some buyers were probably discouraged by their higher prices, for the Trooper had moved distinctly upmarket in its second incarnation.

Nevertheless, the new Troopers quickly established a firm foothold in the market, buyers seeming undeterred by the fact that the new models were considerably thirstier than the old. By way of compensation, the new 3.2-litre V6 petrol engine and 3.1-litre indirect-injection turbodiesel offered more power and greater refinement than their 2.6-litre, four-cylinder and 2.8-litre direct-injection predecessors.

Vital statistics

Engine:	3,165cc injected petrol V6, with 174bhp at 5,200rpm and 192lb.ft at 3,750rpm or 3,059cc indirect-injection intercooled turbodiesel, with 113bhp at 3,400rpm and 192lb.ft at 2,000rpm
Transmission:	Five-speed manual Four-speed automatic optional with petrol engine only Selectable four-wheel drive Automatic freewheeling front hubs Limited-slip differential in rear axle on Duty models
Suspension:	Independent front suspension with twin wishbones and torsion bar springs; live rear axle with trailing links, Panhard rod and coil springs
Steering:	Power-assisted as standard
Brakes:	Ventilated discs front and rear, with standard power assistance; ABS on Citation models
Dimensions:	Wheelbase SWB 91.7in (2,330mm) LWB 108.6in (2,760mm) Length SWB 178.9in (4,545mm) LWB 162in (4,115mm) Height 72in (1,830mm) Width 69in (1,752mm)

The second-generation short-wheelbase Trooper Duty with 3.1-litre turbodiesel engine as introduced into the UK market in 1992.

Ground clearance	SWB 8.5in (215mm)	
	LWB 8.3in (210mm)	
Weight	SWB petrol 3,960lb	
	(1,796kg)	
	SWB diesel 4,190lb	
	(1,900kg)	
	LWB petrol 4,145lb	
	(1,880kg)	
	LWB diesel 4,375lb	
	(1,984kg)	
Number of seats:	SWB 4	
	LWB 5 or 7	
Towing capacity:	6,614lb (3,000kg)	
Insurance rating:	Group 13	
Fuel consumption:	SWB petrol	11–21mpg
	SWB turbodiesel	17–27mpg
	LWB petrol	11–21mpg
	LWB turbodiesel	17–27mpg
Top speed:	SWB petrol	105mph
	SWB turbodiesel	94mph
	LWB petrol	105mph
	LWB turbodiesel	94mph
0–60mph:	SWB petrol	11.5sec
	SWB turbodiesel	16.6sec
	LWB petrol	11.5sec
	LWB turbodiesel	16.6sec

Like the original Trooper, the second-generation model is aesthetically rather uninspiring, although its styling does a good job of disguising increases in size: the second-generation models are longer and taller overall, and have longer wheelbases and wider tracks than their predecessors. That styling is at its happiest on the long-wheelbase five-door estates, and looks distinctly foreshortened on the three-door short-wheelbase models. As before, the UK importers have brought in both types, and short-wheelbase vans for the commercial market as well.

For these new models, Isuzu made good use of their connections with the General Motors empire: the management system of the V6 petrol engine comes from GM in the USA, while the handling was developed with assistance from Lotus in Britain, another GM-owned company at the time that the second-generation Trooper was being prepared for production. However, when GM's Vauxhall division decided to import the Trooper and badge it as a Vauxhall Monterey in 1994, the future of the Isuzu-badged models in Britain was thrown into doubt. In the end, an agreement was reached under which the Trooper will cease to be sold as an Isuzu in Britain after 1997.

The 3.2-litre V6 petrol-engined version of the short-wheelbase Trooper Citation, distinguishable by the 'V6' badge ahead of the front wheelarch and by this model's five-spoke wheels.

The 3.1-litre turbodiesel-engined long-wheelbase Isuzu Trooper is a strong contender at the luxury end of the 4x4 market, the Citation model's specification including air conditioning and leather upholstery.

Character summary

Strangely, character is the one quality that is lacking in what are in most respects impressive vehicles: the styling is bland; the interior trim rather ordinary (although the leather Citation trim improves its appearance); and long acquaintance with a Trooper suggests it is one of those vehicles which does everything expected of it without actually excelling at anything.

The Trooper is a comfortable and relaxing vehicle for long journeys, and top models are very well-equipped with convenience features. The whole bias of its design is towards road use, which certainly makes sense for the long-wheelbase estates but does detract from the functional feel expected by many buyers of short-wheelbase vehicles. In many respects, the second-generation Trooper is a typical product of the early Nineties, when manufacturers were aiming above all to make their 4x4s more car-like. However, the van-like driving position of the Trooper is a constant reminder that this is in fact a dual-purpose off-roader.

Performance summary

The second-generation Troopers are very good road vehicles, offering better acceleration and greater refinement than their predecessors. The turbodiesel engine gives impressive mid-range acceleration, while the petrol V6 is responsive and delivers its power smoothly, especially at the top end where multi-valve engines traditionally excel.

The ride is soft and stable, but the vehicles can wallow if pushed hard. Whereas the petrol-engined models exhibit no vices, the front end of the turbodiesel models seems to bounce on rough roads, a characteristic probably caused by the extra weight of the engine. Steering is not one of the Trooper's better characteristics, becoming light and rather vague at speed. The brakes lack feel but certainly do their job effectively, and the ABS system on Citation models is rather noisy in operation.

Off the road, these Troopers are rather less impressive. Like the first-generation models, they lack sufficient suspension travel at the front for some conditions. Their new engines also lack bottom-end torque as a result of being biased too heavily towards the middle and upper-range torque needed for road use.

Reliability, weaknesses, spares
The build quality of these vehicles is really excellent, even better than that of the first-generation Troopers. So far, they have had a good reliability record, and no weaknesses have become evident.

Key specification changes in the UK
1992 (Feb):   Introduced to UK
1994 (May):   Vauxhall Monterey versions introduced

Nomenclature
Citation   Luxury specification with limited-slip differential in rear axle, leather and air conditioning; lower body panels finished in grey

Duty   Intermediate specification with limited-slip differential in rear axle and electric windows

Resale values
The second-generation Troopers are widely respected and as a result depreciation is low. It is conceivable that resale values will soften slightly when Troopers are no longer available in the UK and the only versions on sale are badged as Vauxhall Montereys. However, Vauxhall dealers expect to supply all essential parts, so there should be no difficulty in running a Trooper after that date.

Further reading
SWB turbodiesel Duty: *Diesel Car*, October 1992
                            Off Road and 4 Wheel Drive, October 1992
                            International Off-Roader, September 1993
                            Off Road and 4 Wheel Drive, December 1994
LWB turbodiesel Citation: *Diesel Car*, December 1992
LWB V6 Duty: *Autocar and Motor*, October 7, 1992
LWB V6 Citation: *International Off-Roader*, September 1992

JEEP CHEROKEE

Background

Jeep is the oldest name in light four-wheel drive vehicles, but it was a very late entrant to the UK market: although small numbers of Jeeps had been imported over the years by specialists, the parent company did not establish its own representation in Britain until 1993.

Chrysler Jeep began by importing right-hand drive versions of their current models, which included the Cherokee. However, what looked like a new vehicle to UK customers was in fact already an elderly design which had been in production since 1984. Its original purpose was to reclaim a share of the American sport-utility compact market from Ford and GM, and it was only much later that the UK arm of Chrysler saw in the Cherokee a competitor for the stylish family 4x4 market then dominated by the Discovery and Shogun.

The Cherokee has, of course, evolved since 1984, although it is still recognizably the same vehicle. Its success in the USA was one of the main reasons why Chrysler decided to buy AMC (who then owned Jeep) in 1987. Their contribution to the vehicle's development has included much better engines.

The Cherokee is unusual in that its chassisless construction enables it to have a lower overall height than most competitors; the body does not sit on a deep chassis frame. This gives it the general appearance – and some of the interior ambience – of a conventional estate car. Some would argue that this is exactly what it is: a four-wheel drive equivalent of the big Volvo estates.

The biggest advantages of the Cherokee are its compact dimensions and, in 4-litre form, its startling road performance. Its biggest disadvantage is a lack of interior space. Until 1995, there was also no turbodiesel option in a market dominated by turbodiesel vehicles. However, with the adoption of an Italian VM engine (related to that once used in the Range Rover), that deficiency has now been remedied. Sales, already strong, will undoubtedly improve.

Character summary

The Cherokee is a stylish and distinctive family 4x4 with car-like character and dimensions which have contributed to its popularity. It makes an excellent everyday vehicle and is comfortable over long distances, although rear seat passengers are less well accommodated than those in front because their access is hindered by narrow doors and the bench seat itself is rather low-set.

The Cherokee's low roofline gives its interior a smaller feel than many of its competitors enjoy, and it certainly is less spacious than many of them: the roof bars are part of the standard specification for very good reasons! There is also very little space for oddments stowage.

The driving position takes some acclimatization, with a long steering column and a nearly vertical dashboard on which the switchgear is poorly located. Fake wood veneer on the more expensive models tends to cheapen rather than enhance the feel of the interior, but otherwise the typically American high levels of standard equipment are impressive.

51

Vital statistics

Engine:	2,464cc injected petrol four-cylinder, with 122bhp at 5,300rpm and 148lb.ft at 3,200rpm or 3,960cc injected petrol six-cylinder, with 184bhp at 4,750rpm and 240lb.ft at 3,950rpm or 2,499cc indirect-injection turbocharged and intercooled four-cylinder diesel, with 116bhp at 4,000rpm and 207lb.ft at 2,000rpm
Transmission:	Five-speed manual on 2.5-litre models Four-speed automatic on 4-litre models Selectable four-wheel drive (Selec-Trac system on 4-litre models, Command-Trac on 2.5-litre petrol and turbodiesel models) Automatic freewheeling front hubs Limited-slip differential in rear axle
Suspension:	Live front axle with coil springs and anti-roll bar; live rear axle with leaf springs and anti-roll bar
Steering:	Power-assisted as standard
Brakes:	Ventilated discs at the front, drums at the rear,

The Jeep Cherokee 4.0 Limited's six-cylinder petrol engine makes it one of the fastest 4x4 estates on the market; automatic transmission is standard.

with standard power assistance
ABS standard on 4-litre models

Dimensions: Wheelbase 101.4in (2,575mm)
Length 166in (4,240mm)
Height 64in (1,623mm)
Width 70.4in (1,790mm)
Ground clearance 8.5in (215mm)
Weight 2.5-litre models 3,193lb
(1,448kg)
4-litre models 3,381lb
(1,533kg)
Turbodiesel models
3,450lb (1,565kg)

Number of seats: 5
Towing capacity: 5,510lb (2,500kg)
Insurance rating: Group 14
Fuel consumption: 2.5-litre models 15–25mpg
4-litre models 11–21mpg
Turbodiesel models 25–27mpg
Top speed: 2.5-litre models 102mph
4-litre models 110mph
Turbodiesel models 102mph
0–60mph: 2.5-litre models 13.5sec
4-litre models 9.5sec
Turbodiesel models 13.1sec

The alternative Cherokee Sport LE with a lower-revving four-cylinder 2.5-litre petrol engine began life as a special edition in 1994.

The Cherokee Limited became available with a 2.5-litre four-cylinder turbodiesel engine early in 1995.

Performance summary

The most striking qualities of the Cherokee are its car-like performance, handling and ride. The suspension can be a little harsh at low speeds, but gives a smooth ride for motorway cruising. Hard cornering in the powerful 4-litre models can sometimes induce disconcerting oversteer, but this can be eliminated by using the full-time four-wheel drive option instead of rear-wheel drive only.

The 4-litre models are very quick for 4x4 vehicles, although the engine's torque peak is high up the rev band and so it must be revved hard to give its best. The 2.5-litre petrol engine gives only average performance, and in fact the turbodiesel is a better bet from most points of view, despite its higher noise levels.

Off the road, the Cherokee is a competent performer, although the 2.5-litre petrol and turbodiesel engines give better control than the high-revving 4-litre for slow-speed manoeuvring. Axle articulation is not particularly good, but the limited-slip differential goes some way to compensate by transferring the drive from a spinning wheel to one which is likely to have traction.

Reliability, weaknesses, spares

Very early examples of the Cherokee (including some of the press demonstrators) had some niggling faults, but Jeep soon resolved those and the Cherokee now has a very good reliability record. No consistent weaknesses have so far emerged, and it is unlikely that they will in a vehicle which has been in production for more than 10 years. Spares are readily available through Chrysler Jeep dealers in the UK.

Key specification changes in the UK

1993 (Jan):   Introduced to UK
1994 (May):   Stealth special edition
1994 (Dec):   2.5 Sport LE became regular model after brief appearance as special edition
1995 (Apr):   Turbodiesel model introduced; all models had larger front seats, stalk-mounted seatbelt catches, redesigned minor switch-gear and wider front wheelarch flares

Nomenclature

Limited	Basic 4-litre and mid-range Turbodiesel models
Limited SE	High-line 4-litre and Turbodiesel models
Sport	Basic 2.5-litre and Turbodiesel models
Sport LE	High-line 2.5-litre and mid-range Turbodiesel models
Stealth	Limited Edition model based on 4-litre Limited

Resale values

Strong demand for new Cherokees has ensured that used examples retain their value well. There is no reason to believe that this position will change in the near future.

Further reading

2.5 Sport: *Off Road and 4 Wheel Drive*, November 1993
               International Off-Roader, August 1994
4.0 Limited: *Off Road and 4 Wheel Drive*, July 1993
               International Off-Roader, May 1993

Automatic transmission on a Cherokee 4.0 Limited being put to the test.

JEEP WRANGLER

Background

Visually, the Jeep Wrangler is the latest incarnation of the war-time Willys Jeep which started it all, but the two vehicles are very different indeed under their similar styling. Whereas the war-time Jeep was uncomfortable, slow and utilitarian, the Wrangler is comfortable, quick (especially in 4-litre form) and (in some versions) positively luxurious. Like its illustrious ancestor, it is also ruggedly built.

One reason for the Wrangler's greater sophistication is that it is built around the same mechanical components as are used in the Cherokee sport-utility, a vehicle of very different pretensions. Previous open Jeeps in the range, right down to the CJ-7 model which gave way to the Wrangler in 1986, had shared their mechanical specification with contemporary military Jeeps.

The original Jeep shape might in fact have been lost forever in the mid-Eighties, because the company had lost the military contract which underpinned its existence (the US Army had switched to the bigger Humvee all-terrain vehicle) and there was some doubt whether civilian sales were enough to justify production. However, a promotional tie-up with the Wrangler jeans company helped the traditional Jeep to remain in production and gave its latest incarnation a new name.

Vital statistics

Engine:	2,464cc injected petrol four-cylinder, with 122bhp at 5,300rpm and 148lb.ft at 3,200rpm or 3,960cc injected petrol six-cylinder, with 184bhp at 4,750rpm and 240lb.ft at 3,950rpm
Transmission:	Five-speed manual or three-speed automatic (4-litre models only) Selectable four-wheel drive (Command-Trac system on all models) Automatic freewheeling front hubs Limited-slip differential in rear axle of 4-litre models
Suspension:	Live axles front and rear, with leaf springs and front anti-roll bar
Steering:	Power-assisted as standard
Brakes:	Ventilated discs at the front, drums at the rear, with standard power assistance

Concave five-spoke alloy wheels identify this as the Wrangler 4.0 Sahara, a high-line model introduced early in 1995.

Dimensions:	Wheelbase	93in (2,373mm)
	Length	153in (3,879mm)
	Height	70in (1,767mm)
	Width	66in (1,676mm)
	Ground clearance	8.1in (205mm)
	Weight	2.5-litre models 3,073lb (1,394kg)
		4-litre models 3,205lb (1,454kg)
Number of seats:	4	
Towing capacity:	2,200lb (1,000kg)	
Insurance rating:	2.5-litre models	Group 12
	4-litre models	Group 14
Fuel consumption:	2.5-litre models	15–25mpg
	4-litre models	11–21mpg
Top speed:	2.5-litre models	95mph
	4-litre models	100mph
0–60mph:	2.5-litre models	13.6sec
	4-litre manual	8.8sec
	4-litre auto	9.5sec

Jeep deliberately retained the traditional separate-chassis construction and military styling for their new vehicle. However, their market research had shown that only some 5 per cent of US buyers actually used their vehicles regularly off-road, and that most Jeeps were used purely as road vehicles. As a result, the Wrangler was built with a greater bias towards road use and convenience features than earlier models of its type. Nevertheless, it retained its traditional off-road ability.

In the UK, the Wrangler is sold with a removable plastic hardtop as standard; a folding soft-top is an extra-cost option. No diesel-engined model is currently available, although the VM turbodiesel fitted to the Cherokee is expected to become available for the Wrangler in continental Europe and may also reach British showrooms.

Character summary

The Wrangler is a two-door vehicle with a removable hardtop, optional soft-top and a padded rollcage. It was never intended as family transport and is unsuited to that role: it is at its best when used as a weekend fun machine. Its traditional (for which read 'old-fashioned') styling is designed to be noticed and to create an image for its owner, and although it can be bought with comfort and convenience features, it is an essentially impractical vehicle.

In base form, the Wrangler is surprisingly spartan for an American leisure product. Its interior is disappointingly utilitarian without the leather option available on Limited models. Nevertheless, it undeniably has a great deal of character – and that is what persuades most of its buyers to have one.

Performance summary

All versions of the Wrangler are easy to drive, with light power-assisted steering and either automatic transmission or a slick five-speed gearbox. The 2.5-litre is quick, while the 4-litre models are very fast – automatic

An open-top Wrangler 4.0 Limited exemplifying the famous Jeep's unique blend of fun and utility.

transmission keeps the power under control rather better than the manual gearbox. The stiff springs make for stable cornering with little body roll, but they also make the ride rather rough, with plenty of pitch and bounce. At motorway speeds, the vehicle suffers quite badly from wind noise even when the hardtop is in place.

Off the road, the Wrangler is not actually as great a performer as its famous name would suggest. The old-fashioned leaf spring suspension is primarily to blame because it does not allow as much axle articulation as more modern coil-sprung designs. Nevertheless, the Wrangler does acquit itself well off the road – perhaps rather better with the 2.5-litre engine than with the more road-oriented 4-litre.

Reliability, weaknesses, spares
Build quality is rather variable on the Wrangler, but no consistent weaknesses have shown up since the model has been imported into the UK. It is unlikely that they will, as the design is now nearly 10 years old and any early difficulties must have been sorted out many years ago. However, it is worth checking used examples to see if the front safety-belt webbing has become damaged after getting caught in the door locks.

Spares are readily available through the Chrysler Jeep dealership network.

Key specification changes in the UK
1993 (Jan):   Range introduced to UK
1994 (Mar):   Automatic option with 4-litre engine
1995 (Feb):   Sahara model replaced Limited as high-line variant of 4-litre

Nomenclature
Limited   1993–1995, 4-litre high-line model, with leather upholstery, cross-spoke alloy wheels, etc
Sahara   1995 on, 4-litre high-line model, distinguished by concave five-spoke alloy wheels
Sport   2.5-litre model

Resale values
The Jeep Wrangler is nothing like as popular as its Cherokee stablemate in Britain, but so far resale values are holding up well.

Further reading
2.5-litre: *Off Road and 4 Wheel Drive*, June 1993
        International Off-Roader, May 1993
4-litre Automatic: *Off Road and 4 Wheel Drive*, June 1994

LADA NIVA

Background

The Lada Niva was designed for heavy-duty use in the inhospitable regions of the former Soviet Union during the Seventies, and was only later adapted as a fun and leisure vehicle to suit European market trends in the Eighties and Nineties. With that in mind, it is easier to understand the background to this vehicle, which is quite a remarkable one in many ways.

The most interesting features of the Niva are its chassisless construction (still rare in the 4x4 world) and the fact that it came with permanent four-wheel drive and coil spring suspension at a time when only the Range Rover offered such features. Its low cost quickly helped it to achieve popularity in Britain, and the importers have also offered van versions alongside the standard three-door estate.

The first Nivas to reach the UK were left-hand drive examples, which were imported as long ago as 1978. Some were converted to right-hand drive in

---

Vital statistics

Engine:	1,568cc four-cylinder carburettor petrol, with 78bhp at 5,400rpm and 88lb.ft at 3,000rpm
Transmission:	Four-speed manual (to 1985) or five-speed manual (1985 on) Permanent four-wheel drive Lockable centre differential
Suspension:	Independent front suspension with coil springs and anti-roll bar Live rear axle with coil springs, four locating arms and transverse rod
Steering:	Unassisted
Brakes:	Discs at the front, drums at the rear
Dimensions:	Wheelbase 88in (2,235mm) Length 147in (3,734mm) Height 65in (1,650mm) Width 66in (1,677mm) Ground clearance 9.3in (236mm) Weight 2,535lb (1,150kg)
Number of seats:	4
Towing capacity:	3,472lb (1,575kg)
Insurance rating:	Group 8
Fuel consumption:	22–30mpg
Top speed:	82mph (five-speed)
0–60mph:	22sec

The Niva Cossack has always been a highly decorated model; this was the treatment offered in 1990, complete with matching front and rear bull bars.

Britain, but imports of right-hand drive models did not begin until 1983. To improve the Niva's market image (always handicapped by its association with the Lada cars which are the butt of so many jokes), the importers followed up with the better-equipped Cossack model, which featured a number of UK-sourced parts. A soft-top model, converted in Greece, was also briefly available in the mid-Eighties.

The Niva's biggest advantages are that it is cheap to buy and able off the road; its biggest disadvantages are its build quality, some aspects of its design and its lack of refinement on the road. Despite the age of the design and some serious drawbacks, it continues to sell a few hundred examples every year, and the UK importers have shown an improved 'Mark III' model which might go on sale later.

Character summary
The Niva is a small three-door 4x4 with the limited luggage space typical of short-wheelbase vehicles. It is a rather crude vehicle in many ways, with little refinement, a rather old-fashioned facia design and a cheap-looking interior. Passenger space in the rear is limited, and the standard vinyl-covered seats are not very comfortable; the UK-sourced items in Cossack models are very much better.

Noise at speed makes the Niva unsuitable for long-distance work, although it is perfectly acceptable as a town runabout. Its limited towing capacity makes it unsuitable for large trailers or caravans. Owners also have to endure niggling design shortcomings – such as the need to remove the bull bar on early Cossack models in order to change a headlamp bulb. The vehicle is

The Niva Cossack underwent considerable modernization in 1992 and reappeared with this striking paint treatment on the sides.

probably best bought for recreational off-road use and short road journeys only.

Performance summary

The Niva is not particularly pleasant to drive on the road; even the refinements introduced in 1993 did not transform its overall character. It suffers from vague and heavy steering, a notchy gearchange, uncommunicative brakes and an awkward driving position. Its Fiat-designed engine is capable of propelling the vehicle at over 80mph, but most drivers find 65mph a comfortable maximum because of the high noise levels. Overtaking can be a slow and risky business as the engine lacks high-speed torque. There is also a lot of body roll in cornering. However, the ride quality is reasonably good, in spite of the vehicle's short wheelbase.

Where the Niva comes into its own is off the road – the environment for which it was designed. Its small engine delivers enough torque for most situations, the short wheelbase, minimal overhangs and high ground clearance prevent fouling, and the long travel suspension gives both good axle articulation and a fairly comfortable ride on rough tracks.

Reliability, weaknesses, spares

The build quality of the Niva is poor, with rough edges and exposed metal in the interior, and poor detail finish in many areas. Build quality was improved in 1993, but is still not up to Western standards or expectations. Some of the Russian-made consumables (such as wiper blades) are of poor quality and are best replaced with European equivalents.

Rust is to be expected in the body seams of older vehicles, under the bright trim and around windows. The gearchange becomes sloppy with age and the catch on the Cossack's swingaway spare-wheel mount is often ineffective. Even new vehicles may suffer from water leaks. Worth knowing is that reconditioned engines are not available and that an expensive new power unit is likely to be the only solution to a major engine failure – which is fortunately rare.

Nivas tend to suffer from many irritating faults which do not actually disable the vehicle. Mechanical reliability, however, is very good. This is perhaps fortunate, because spares can sometimes take several weeks to arrive through Lada dealers.

Key specification changes in the UK

1983 (Mar):	Available in RHD
1985 (Oct):	Five-speed gearbox replaced four-speed
1986 (May):	Cossack introduced
1992 (Jun):	Cossack modernized and upgraded
1993 (Jun):	All models benefited from changes to improve refinement levels; new side decals for base models and Cossack; side steps and roof rails standardized on Cossack

Nomenclature

Cossack	High-line model, with better seats, alloy wheels, bull bar, glass sunroof, extra lamps, wheelarch extensions, etc
Cossack Cabrio	Soft-top conversion, available only briefly in 1986

A recent example of the Niva in standard trim, with a minimum of side decoration and steel rather than alloy wheels.

Resale values

Although the Niva does hold its value better than Lada cars, depreciation is heavy. Early examples can now be bought for a few hundred pounds. The less common Cossack models are generally more desirable and therefore hold their value better than the base Niva.

Club information

There are no fewer than four clubs for Niva owners in the UK:

Lada Niva Owners' Club
David Woodman
103 Offa
Lodge Vale Park
Chirk
Nr Wrexham
(01691-777252)

Lada Niva South-East Owners' Club
Paul Sutton
163 Borough Road
Petersfield
Hants GU32 3LP
(01730-263911)

National Niva Owners' Club
Geraint Rowlands
Golwyg-y-Myndd
8 Cleveland Avenue
Tywyn
Gwynedd LL36 9EG

National Niva Owners' Club (Scotland)
Iain McLean
Thistle Flat
Plumscarden
Elgin
Moray IV30 3US

Further reading

All models:	*Off Road and 4 Wheel Drive*, November 1991
	Off Road and 4 Wheel Drive, May 1993
	International Off-Roader, July 1994
Cossack:	*Off Road and 4 Wheel Drive*, August 1986
	International Off-Roader, October 1994
Revised '93 models:	*Off Road and 4 Wheel Drive*, August 1993

LAND ROVER 88 AND 109 COUNTY STATION WAGONS

Background

There have been Land Rover Station Wagons of one sort or another for more than 40 years, and the basic shape of the vehicles familiar today was established as long ago as 1958. However, the early Land Rover Station Wagon was designed more as an expedition and dirt-road vehicle than as dual-purpose, everyday transport. It was not until 1982 that the basic vehicles were upgraded with the more refined County specification options. Most Station Wagons sold in the UK after that date were County types.

By the time the County Station Wagons were introduced, the Land Rover had been around in Series III guise for 11 years, so the basic design was already quite old-fashioned. It consisted of a traditional ladder-frame chassis, with a separate body panelled in corrosion-resistant aluminium alloy. The chassis came in two wheelbase lengths, and the Station Wagons could accommodate either seven passengers (on the 88-inch wheelbase) or 12 passengers (on the 109-inch wheelbase). However, the 12-seater model was more accurately a 10-seater and was sold as such outside the UK, where tax laws dictated the notional 12 seats.

Most County Station Wagons have four-cylinder engines of 2.25-litre capacity, either petrol or diesel. However, the 109-inch County Station Wagon

The County station wagon based on the Land Rover 88in short-wheelbase chassis is a compact and versatile go-anywhere vehicle.

could also be bought with a 3.5-litre V8 petrol engine (a detuned version of the contemporary Range Rover engine), which greatly improves the road performance. The V8-powered models have permanent four-wheel drive; all others have selectable four-wheel drive.

The long-wheelbase County Station Wagons were replaced by the One Ten County models in 1983, and the short-wheelbase models gave way to the Ninety County during 1984. Many County-type vehicles have subsequently been created by fitting County parts to ordinary Station Wagons, and there is a thriving business in Britain of revitalizing older Land Rovers in this way. Such rebuilds often use parts from the newer Ninety and One Ten Land Rovers. They can generally be recognized quite easily because very few rebuilders use the original brown or red paint and low-key cream side stripes of the genuine Series III County: most prefer brighter colours and the more garish side stripes associated with later models.

Vital statistics

Engine:	2,286cc four-cylinder carburettor petrol, with 77bhp at 4,250rpm and 124lb.ft at 2,500rpm or 3,528cc V8-cylinder carburettor petrol, with 91bhp at 3,500rpm and 166lb.ft at 2,000rpm (109-inch models only) or 2,286cc four-cylinder indirect-injection diesel, with 62bhp at 4,000rpm and 103lb.ft at 1,800rpm
Transmission:	Four-speed manual Selectable four-wheel drive (four-cylinder models) Permanent four-wheel drive (V8 models)
Suspension:	Live front and rear axles; semi-elliptic leaf springs all round
Steering:	Unassisted
Brakes:	Drum brakes all round with standard power assistance

Dimensions:		
	Wheelbase	SWB 88in (2,235mm)
		LWB 109in (2,768mm)
	Length	SWB 142.6in (3,622mm)
		LWB 175in (4,445mm)
	Height	SWB 77in (1,955mm)
		LWB 79in (2,006mm)
	Width	66in
	Ground clearance	SWB 8in (203mm)
		LWB 9.75in (248mm)

It is more or less standard practice for Land Rover owners in Britain to modify or personalize their vehicles in some way, and there is a large and thriving aftermarket industry to cater for this. It is therefore rare to find a vehicle in completely original, ex-showroom, condition.

Character summary

The Land Rover County Station Wagons are rugged and characterful vehicles, but they are essentially adapted utility models and their characteristics must be seen in that light. Instrumentation and controls are van-like, and the moulded plastic dashboard is crude and offers no secure oddments storage. Seating is basic and the inward-facing seats in the rear (four in SWB models, six in LWB models) are not at all comfortable for long journeys. Opening windows are sliding rather than winding types, fresh-air ventilation is by means of simple flaps (with fly-screens) and even the outside door handles are crude and basic.

Weight	SWB petrol 3,365lb (1,526kg)	
	SWB diesel 3,456lb (1,567kg)	
	LWB petrol 4-cyl 3,976lb (1,803kg)	
	LWB petrol V8 4,080lb (1,850kg)	
	LWB diesel 4,059lb (1,841kg)	
Number of seats:	SWB 7	
	LWB 12	
Towing capacity:	4,400lb (2,000kg)	
Insurance rating:	Group 5	
Fuel consumption:	SWB petrol	18mpg
	SWB diesel	25mpg
	LWB petrol 4-cyl	16mpg
	LWB petrol V8	17mpg
	LWB diesel	24mpg
Top speed:	SWB petrol	70mph
	SWB diesel	60mph
	LWB petrol	4-cyl 68mph
	LWB petrol	V8 76mph
	LWB diesel	60mph
0–60mph:	SWB petrol	29sec
	SWB diesel	32sec
	LWB petrol	4-cyl 30sec
	LWB petrol	V8 27sec
	LWB diesel	34sec

Genuine original County station wagons based on the 109in long-wheelbase chassis are a rare breed and consequently highly sought after.

The long-wheelbase models can feel large and cumbersome, especially in town driving, but the short-wheelbase types are quite manoeuvrable. Steering is not unduly heavy, but once again reveals the vehicles' utilitarian origins.

Nevertheless, the Land Rover County Station Wagons undeniably have character, and it is this and their renowned longevity and toughness which attract buyers. They also make excellent towing vehicles, the long-wheelbase types being especially stable.

Performance summary
The chassis on these vehicles dates in its essentials back to 1948, and its road behaviour is not at all sophisticated. The leaf-sprung suspension is firm and the short-wheelbase models give a particularly uncomfortable ride, characterized by pitch and bounce. The gearchange is slow and even the V8 petrol engine cannot persuade one of these vehicles to accelerate very quickly.

Maximum speeds are only barely adequate for modern motoring conditions and the diesel models are frustrating to drive on motorways. Noise levels are also high, and even the optional overdrive (which does help fuel consumption slightly) does not reduce the mechanical din to acceptable levels at speed.

Off the road, these models are excellent performers, outclassed only by more modern coil-sprung vehicles with greater axle articulation. The short-wheelbase models are particularly able off-roaders, while the bottom-end torque of the 109 V8s makes them the best of the long-wheelbase types.

Reliability, weaknesses, spares
The County Station Wagons are reliable old workhorses, and even in old age (the youngest of them is now 11 years old) they are not likely to succumb to inexplicable failures unless they have been poorly maintained. All the

mechanical components are simply designed and the ready availability of spare parts and servicing expertise (primarily outside the main dealerships) means that ownership should present no real problems.

However, the vehicles can be affected by rust in the chassis, most commonly around the outriggers to which the body is mounted, and around the rearmost spring shackles on long-wheelbase models. The rear chassis crossmember can also rust and should be checked carefully if a vehicle is to be used for towing. Body panels dent easily and the steel elements of the inner body can rust; troublespots include the front footwells and the front door pillars.

Diesel engines become smoky after high mileages and their cylinder heads can crack. The V8 petrol engines can also become extremely thirsty if their twin carburettors wear or go out of tune and neglected oil changes will lead to valve-gear rattle. Oil leaks are also not uncommon, particularly from the rear of the engine.

Key specification changes in the UK
1982 (Apr):	County Station Wagons introduced
1983 (Mar):	LWB models replaced by One Ten County
1984 (Jun):	SWB models replaced by Ninety County

Resale values
The age of all these vehicles makes them fairly cheap to buy, although professionally refurbished examples (of which there are many) can cost two or three times as much as a well-used original model. In general, resale values of original vehicles are unlikely to drop significantly below their present levels

The bold rectangular grille immediately identifies this Land Rover station wagon as being powered by the Rover 3.5-litre V8 petrol engine.

until the vehicles become unroadworthy, but refurbished examples are subject to average rates of depreciation.

Club information
Owners of these Land Rovers can join the Land Rover Series III Club, which can be contacted through:

Frank King
16 Holly Street
Cannock
Staffordshire WS11 2RU

In addition, there are many regional Land Rover clubs in Britain, which exist largely to promote off-road driving activities. A full list can be found in magazines such as *Land Rover Owner* and *Land Rover World*.

Further reading
All models: *International Off-Roader*, May 1993
LWB V8:   *Autocar*, November 6, 1982

The popularity of the County specification is such that many owners of earlier, standard-trim station wagons have subsequently had them upgraded to County specification. This diesel-engined Series III, based on the 109in wheelbase chassis, has been immaculately reconditioned and converted by the Land Rover Centre in Huddersfield.

LAND ROVER AND DEFENDER 90 AND 110 COUNTY STATION WAGONS

Background

The Land Rover 90 (Ninety) and 110 (One Ten) were phased in over 1983–1984 to take over from the long-serving Series III models, and they brought with them County Station Wagon variants. They represented a huge advance over the Series III models because they had coil spring suspension instead of leaf springs to improve the ride, and disc front brakes to improve their stopping ability. These Land Rovers were distinguished visually by a flush front, one-piece windscreen and wheelarch 'eyebrows' to cover their wider-track axles. Otherwise, they looked much the same as Land Rovers had done since their 1958 restyle.

It was the long-wheelbase One Ten (with 110 inches between axle centres) which appeared first, replacing the Series III 109 in 1983. The Ninety arrived just over a year later to replace the Series III 88, and actually had a wheelbase of 92.9 inches rather than the 90 inches its name suggested.

It had never been Land Rover policy to make annual changes to its utility models, but as the County Station Wagons were selling to a more fashion-conscious market than the basic utilities, an exception was made. In addition to the changes which affected all Land Rover Station Wagons, County models gained new side decals from time to time to keep them looking fresh.

Like their predecessors, the new County models came with four-cylinder petrol and diesel engines, or a V8 petrol type. The diesel engine's capacity was enlarged in 1984, the four-cylinder petrol type followed suit in 1985 and the V8 was uprated in 1986. That year, the existing diesel was replaced by a turbocharged type. For the first year of production, four-cylinder One Tens were available with selectable four-wheel drive, but the permanent four-wheel drive always fitted to V8 models was then standardized.

In 1990, the Ninety and One Ten were replaced by the Defender 90 and 110, which were simply evolutionary models wearing new badging. The key change which came with Defender models was that the old turbodiesel engine was replaced by a detuned version of the 200Tdi turbodiesel from the Discovery. The V8 remained available, and until 1994 so did the four-cylinder petrol engine. From 1995, however, all Defenders for the British market had Tdi engines unless to special order. From March 1994, the 200Tdi engine was replaced by the quieter 300Tdi type, now in full 111bhp Discovery tune, and a much slicker five-speed gearbox was introduced. Neither the original 90s and 110s nor the Defender models have ever been available with automatic transmission.

The Land Rover 90 County with side decoration as offered in 1984, when the power choice was between 2.3-litre petrol and diesel engines.

Vital statistics

Engine: 2,286cc four-cylinder carburettor petrol, with 74bhp at 4,000rpm and 120lb.ft at 2,000rpm (1983–1985)
or 2,286cc four-cylinder indirect-injection diesel, with 62bhp at 4,000rpm and 103lb.ft at 1,500rpm (1983–1984)
or 2,494cc four-cylinder carburettor petrol, with 83bhp at 4,000rpm and 133lb.ft at 2,000rpm (1985–1986)
or 2,494cc four-cylinder indirect-injection diesel, with 67bhp at 4,000rpm and 114lb.ft at 1,800rpm (1984–1986)
or 2,494cc four-cylinder turbocharged indirect-injection diesel, with 85bhp at 4,000rpm and 150lb.ft at 1,800rpm (1986–1990)
or 3,528cc V8 carburettor petrol, with 114bhp at 4,000rpm and 185lb.ft at 2,500rpm (1983–1986)
or 3,528cc V8 carburettor petrol, with 134bhp at 5,000rpm and 187lb.ft at 2,500rpm (1986–1994)

or 2,495cc four-cylinder turbocharged and inter-cooled direct-injection diesel, with 107bhp at 3,800rpm and 188lb.ft at 1,800rpm (1990–1994) or 2,495cc four-cylinder turbocharged and intercooled direct-injection diesel, with 111bhp at 4,000rpm and 195lb.ft at 1,800rpm (1994 on)

Transmission: Five-speed manual (four-speed on 1983–1985 One Ten V8)
Permanent four-wheel drive (selectable four-wheel drive optional on 1983–1984 One Ten four-cylinder models)

Suspension: Live front and rear axles; coil springs all round. Front axle has radius arms and a Panhard rod; rear axle has radius arms and an A-frame; LWB models have a self-levelling strut on the rear axle

Steering: Power-assisted as standard

Brakes: Discs on the front wheels; drums at the rear (1983–1994) or discs at the rear (1994 on)

Dimensions:

Wheelbase	SWB 92.9in (2,360mm)	
	LWB 110in (2,794mm)	
Length	SWB 146.5in (3,721mm)	
	LWB 180.3in (4,580mm)	
Height	SWB 77.3in (1,963mm)	
	LWB 80.1in (2,034mm)	
Width	70.5in (1,791mm)	
Ground clearance	SWB 7.5in (190mm)	
	LWB 8.5in (215mm)	
Weight	SWB petrol 4-cyl 3,768lb (1,709kg)	
	SWB petrol V8 3,750lb (1,701kg)	
	SWB diesel and turbodiesel 3,850lb (1,746kg)	
	SWB Defender Tdi 3,957lb (1,795kg)	
	LWB petrol 4-cyl 4,182lb (1,897kg)	
	LWB petrol V8 4,127lb (1,872kg)	
	LWB diesel and turbodiesel 4,268lb (1,936kg)	
	LWB Defender Tdi 4,530lb (2,055kg)	

Number of seats:	SWB 7	
	LWB 12	
Towing capacity:	8,800lb (3,990kg)	
Insurance rating:	Group 5 (2.25-litre and 2.5-litre models except Diesel Turbo)	
	Group 7 (all other models)	
Fuel consumption:	SWB petrol 4-cyl	19mpg
	SWB petrol V8	13–15mpg
	SWB diesel	22mpg
	SWB turbodiesel	18mpg
	SWB Defender Tdi	25mpg
	LWB petrol 4-cyl	17mpg
	LWB petrol V8	13–14mpg
	LWB diesel	22mpg
	LWB turbodiesel	20mpg
	LWB Defender Tdi	23mpg
Top speed:	SWB petrol 4-cyl	72mph
	SWB petrol V8	85mph (114bhp) or 90mph (134bhp)
	SWB diesel	68mph
	SWB turbodiesel	75mph
	SWB Defender Tdi	85mph
	LWB petrol 4-cyl	70mph
	LWB petrol V8	78mph (114bhp) or 85mph (134bhp)
	LWB diesel	62mph
	LWB turbodiesel	70mph
	LWB Defender Tdi	83mph
0–60mph:	SWB petrol 4-cyl	18sec
	SWB petrol V8	14.5sec (114bhp) or 13.5sec (134bhp)
	SWB diesel	26sec
	SWB turbodiesel	22.5sec
	SWB Defender Tdi	21sec
	LWB petrol 4-cyl	19sec
	LWB petrol V8	16.5sec (114bhp) or 15.1sec (134bhp)
	LWB diesel	28sec
	LWB turbodiesel	23sec
	LWB Defender Tdi	22sec

Character summary

These Land Rovers are still essentially load-luggers rather than stylish 4x4s, even though their coil-spring suspension makes them very much more comfortable than their predecessors. Their character is quite different from that of the stylish family-oriented 4x4 estates, and despite the fairly comfortable level of appointments they always tend to feel like rugged workhorses.

Short-wheelbase models make quite good urban runabouts, but the long-wheelbase models are too big for some types of town work – even the standard power-assisted steering cannot make them physically smaller for manoeuvring in confined spaces. For long-distance motorway work, only those models with the V8 petrol engine or Defenders with the 200 Tdi and 300 Tdi turbodiesels can really be recommended. Worth remembering is that the 300 Tdi is much quieter than the 200 Tdi, which can be a gruff and raucous engine.

However, these vehicles are undeniably characterful, the Defender 110 County Tdi offering a particularly satisfying blend of rugged strength, refinement and economy.

Performance summary
If acceleration and high cruising speeds are important, the only examples of these Land Rovers to go for are those with V8 petrol or Tdi diesel engines. All the others are rather disappointingly slow, the long-wheelbase naturally-aspirated diesels being the worst offenders in this respect.

Ride quality is generally very good; brakes and steering are also very much better than on earlier Land Rovers. However, the gearchange can be poor: it is vague on early four-speed One Tens, rather agricultural on five-speed pre-Defender V8 models and can be baulky when cold on all other five-speeds built before March 1994 (when the much slicker R380 gearbox was introduced).

Sturdy and workmanlike, the 110 County station wagon with its coil-spring suspension offers a much more comfortable ride than its predecessors.

Another variation in side decoration identifies this first version of the vehicle formerly known as the Land Rover 110 County station wagon after it had been given its new Defender name in 1990.

Reliability, weaknesses, spares
Build quality is not consistent, and even brand-new vehicles sometimes suffer from small but irritating faults. The aluminium alloy body panels dent just as easily as those on earlier Land Rovers, and there may still be rust in the windscreen pillars and front footwells. Water leaks are a common source of annoyance.

However, these are generally sturdy and reliable vehicles once teething troubles have been sorted out. Servicing expertise and spares are readily available from Land Rover franchised dealers or from the large number of aftermarket and non-franchised specialists in the UK.

Key specification changes in the UK
1983 (Mar):   One Ten County introduced
1984 (Jan):   2.5-litre diesel engine replaced 2.25-litre
1984 (Jun):   Selectable four-wheel drive option deleted
1985 (May):   Five-speed gearbox replaced four-speed type in One Ten County
1985 (Aug):   2.5-litre petrol engine replaced 2.25-litre
1986 (Oct):   Turbodiesel engine replaced naturally-aspirated type in all County models; power increase for V8 petrol engine; 4-cyl petrol engine deleted
1987 (Dec):   Cosmetic changes with black bumpers and body-colour grille; glass sunroof added
1988 (Dec):   Ribless roof and rivet-free upper rear body sides introduced

| 1990 (Sep): | Original range replaced by Defender models; 200 Tdi direct-injection engine replaced turbodiesel; no 90 County available |
| 1994 (Mar): | 300 Tdi engine replaced 200 Tdi type and repositioned in engine bay; all petrol models deleted (except to special order); 90 County reinstated |

Nomenclature

Defender	Post-1990 models
Diesel Turbo	1986–1990 models with turbodiesel engine
Tdi	Post-1990 models with 200 Tdi or 300 Tdi direct-injection turbodiesel engines

Resale values

Resale values of the coil-sprung County Station Wagons are generally strong. The Tdi-powered Defenders are particularly sought after on the used market and will probably continue to be a good bet for many years. Among older vehicles, the V8 petrol types hold their value better than other varieties.

Early examples of these models are often professionally refurbished in exactly the same way as their Series III counterparts: their bolt-together construction allows elements of later vehicles to be grafted onto earlier types with a minimum of difficulty. Professionally reconditioned vehicles will inevitably command much higher prices than well-used originals of the same age, but they will, of course, be subject to levels of depreciation similar to those of a brand-new vehicle.

The traditional Land Rover was given the Defender name (to distinguish it from the Discovery) in September 1990. This is the 90 station wagon, initially powered by the 2.5-litre four-cylinder 200Tdi turbodiesel engine and from 1994 by the much quieter 300Tdi derivative.

Club information

These Land Rovers are welcomed by the large number of regional Land Rover clubs in Britain, which exist largely to promote off-road driving activities. A full list can be found in magazines such as *Land Rover Owner* and *Land Rover World*.

Further reading

90, all models: *Off Road and 4 Wheel Drive*, June 1993
90 Diesel Turbo: *Diesel Car*, September 1989
90 V8:   *Autocar and Motor*, February 22, 1989
110 V8:   *Autocar and Motor*, December 9, 1987
Defender 90 Tdi   *Land Rover World*, September 1994
Defender 110 Tdi: *Diesel Car*, January 1991
90 and 110 D/Turbo: *Off Road and 4 Wheel Drive*, November 1986

These days the Defender no longer carries the Land Rover name across the top of the radiator grille, only on a discreet badge towards the base of the grille. This is a 1993 version of the turbodiesel-powered 110 station wagon; the alternative power unit was the 3.5-litre Rover V8 petrol engine, which from 1995 has only been available in Defenders to special order.

LAND ROVER DISCOVERY

Background

Land Rover developed the Discovery as a competitor to the Japanese family 4x4s which had the market largely to themelves in the later Eighties. The vehicle was launched in 1989, initially in three-door form; the five-door followed in 1990 and soon became the more popular variant. Unusually, both three-door and five-door variants share the same wheelbase and overall dimensions.

The Discovery has been Britain's most popular 4x4 throughout the early Nineties, and is also a strong seller overseas. One of the keys to its success is its harmonious blend of practical family estate with the standard 4x4 strengths of ruggedness, spaciousness and towing ability. Its biggest drawback is the raised rear roof which provides headroom for passengers in the occasional rear seats, as this makes the vehicle too tall for many multi-storey car parks and domestic garages.

The Discovery is built on the chassis of the first-generation Range Rover and shares much of its mechanical specification. There are also commercial (van) versions of the Discovery based on the three-door body, and a few examples have been stretched as the basis of ambulance conversions.

Although the Land Rover Discovery was initially launched in three-door form in 1989, the five-door version soon followed and became the more popular version. This example is powered by the 2.5-litre turbodiesel engine.

Character summary

The Land Rover Discovery is essentially a family 4x4, even though the original three-door models were promoted with a 'lifestyle' image closer to that of short-wheelbase three-door models from other manufacturers. Its design majors on practicality and on driveability, one of the design aims being to make the change from a conventional 4x2 estate car easy, especially for women drivers.

The Discovery's interior has a versatile layout, with split-folding rear seats to give maximum loadspace versatility and folding inward-facing rear seats (not on all models). Stowage space for oddments is good, with roof nets, door pockets and flat surfaces on dashboard and console; however, some stowage spaces are not as useful as promotional material suggests.

From the beginning, the Discovery was marketed with a wide variety of

---

Vital statistics

Engine:	3,528cc carburettor petrol V8, with 144bhp at 5,000rpm and 192lb.ft at 2,800rpm (1989–1990) or 3,528cc injected petrol V8, with 163bhp at 4,750rpm and 212lb.ft at 2,600rpm (1990–1992) or 3,528cc injected petrol V8, with 153bhp at 4,750rpm and 192lb.ft at 2,600rpm (1992–1993, and earlier models with catalyst) or 3,947cc injected petrol V8, with 180bhp at 4,750rpm and 230lb.ft at 3,100rpm (1993 on) or 2,495cc turbocharged and intercooled diesel four-cylinder, with 111bhp at 4,000rpm and 195lb.ft at 1,800rpm or 1,994cc injected petrol four-cylinder, with 134bhp at 6,000rpm and 137lb.ft at 2,500rpm (1993 on)
Transmission:	Five-speed manual (improved in 1994) or four-speed automatic Permanent four-wheel drive with lockable centre differential
Suspension:	Live front and rear axles; coil springs all round. Front axle has radius arms and a Panhard rod; rear axle has radius arms and an A-frame. Anti-roll bars on front axle optional from 1992 (retro-fit possible) and standard from 1994
Steering:	Power-assisted as standard

accessories and optional extras which allowed owners to personalize their vehicles. Many of these are designed to promote an image, and the Discovery rates highly in such stakes. It also has a very powerful appeal as a sensible but stylish family 4x4.

Performance summary

The Discovery has good on-road performance, with even the slowest models (five-door automatic turbodiesels) being acceptable for most purposes. The Mpi models with their four-cylinder petrol engines are not popular in the UK, and were in fact designed mainly for export markets; their engines lack the muscularity which is part of the Discovery's image, and their fuel economy is not significantly better than that of the V8 petrol models.

The most rapid performance comes from the 3.9-litre V8i versions with

Brakes:	Discs on all four wheels, with power assistance as standard	
Dimensions:	Wheelbase	100in (2,540mm)
	Length	178in (4,521mm)
	Height	75.6in (1,920mm)
	Width	70.6in (1,793mm)
	Weight	4,158–4,257lb (1,885–1,930kg), depending on model
Number of seats:	5 standard; 7 optional	
Towing capacity:	7,700lb (3,500kg) except Mpi at 6,050lb (2,750kg)	
Insurance rating:	2-litre models	Group 11
	2.5-litre models	Group 12
	3.5-litre models	Group 13
Fuel consumption:	V8	14–20mpg
	V8i 3.5	16–18mpg
	V8i 3.9	17–23mpg
	Mpi	20–23mpg
	Tdi	24–32mpg
Top speed:	V8	99mph
	V8i 3.5	105mph
	V8i 3.9	106mph
	Mpi	98mph
	Tdi	92mph
0–60mph:	V8	13sec
	V8i 3.5	12sec
	V8i 3.9	9sec (automatic 13sec)
	Mpi	15sec
	Tdi	17sec

manual gearboxes, but the nicest to drive are automatic 3.9-litre models – and these are only marginally slower than manual models. Most popular by a very long chalk, however, are the turbodiesel models. Their biggest drawback is engine noise (much improved in models with the 300 Tdi engine), but their excellent fuel economy more than compensates and their mid-range acceleration is good enough for most situations.

The Discovery is both spacious and comfortable. However, the front seats in pre-1994 models can feel a little hard, while the inward-facing rear seats are not suitable for those over about 5ft 8in tall. The ride quality is excellent, and handling – especially with the anti-roll bars – very reassuring. Good stability, permanent four-wheel drive and plenty of low-down torque (except in the Mpi) make the Discovery a first-rate towing vehicle.

Off-road, the Discovery is a superb performer. The long-travel coil spring suspension allows a comfortable ride over rough surfaces. It also gives huge axle articulation, which allows the vehicle to retain traction in situations which would defeat many competitive vehicles. The permanent four-wheel drive is another off-roading bonus.

Reliability, weaknesses, spares
The Discovery has generally proved extremely reliable in service. Spares are available through the large Land Rover dealer network. Some consumables

A 1992 3.5-litre V8 petrol-engined Discovery with three-door bodywork; the V8i badge ahead of the driver's door confirms that, unlike the earliest Discoverys, this vehicle's engine is fuel-injected rather than carburettor-fed.

The Discovery underwent a facelift in 1994 including a revised grille, standard anti-roll bars, an improved manual gearbox and uprated interior.

and accessories are also available from non-franchised outlets.

Nevertheless, there are some weaknesses to look for. Very early examples sometimes suffered from worn hinges on the rear tailgate and from rust on that panel. Noisy valve gear on the V8 engines results from neglect of oil changes (or from low oil levels when the engine uses or leaks oil), and vibration on the 200 Tdi engines can cause fuel pipe unions to loosen and leak. Problems with engine starting and tuning on injected V8 petrol models may be caused by problems with the ECU (the engine's computer 'brain'), which is expensive to replace.

Key specification changes in the UK
1989: Three-door model introduced, with 3.5-litre V8 carburettor or 200Tdi intercooled turbodiesel engine
1990: Five-door model announced. Carburettor V8 replaced by fuel-injected type; petrol models renamed V8i
1991: Improved gearbox synchromesh
1992: Four-speed automatic option for V8i models; Freestyle option (alloy wheels with 235/70 tyres, anti-rollbars)
1993: Mpi (2-litre petrol) engine announced for 3-door and 5-door models; automatic option for Tdi models; 3.9-litre injected V8 replaced 3.5-litre type
1994: Facelifted models with new front end, new 'airbag' dashboard and rear lights in bumper; quieter 300 Tdi turbodiesel replaced 200 Tdi type; improved R380 manual gearbox replaced LT77S type; ABS and airbag options; top-specification ES model introduced; anti-roll bars standardized

Nomenclature

ES   High-line models, post-1994, with leather upholstery, air conditioning, enamelled five-spoke wheels, etc
Mpi   Models with 2-litre petrol engine
Tdi   Models with 200 Tdi or 300 Tdi turbodiesel engines
V8   Models with V8 carburettor engine
V8i   Models with injected 3.5-litre or 3.9-litre V8 engines

Resale values

Depreciation on Discovery models is low and demand is high. Three-door models are perceived as less desirable than five-doors and will be correspondingly harder to sell on. The least desirable models are the carburetted three-door V8s and the Mpi variants; these suffer the highest depreciation. Best buys are 3.9-litre V8i five-doors, either manual or automatic, and five-door Tdi models (the later the better, as refinement has been improved over the years).

Club information

The Discovery has its own – small – owners' club, Club Discovery, which operates from:

West Farm
Witham-on-the-Hill
Bourne
Lincolnshire PE10 0JN
(Tel: 01778-33-275/484)

Further reading

All models:	*Off Road and 4 Wheel Drive*, August 1993
	International Off-Roader, August 1994
V8 3-door:	*Autocar and Motor*, January 3,1990
V8i (3.5) 3-door:	*Autocar and Motor*, October 17, 1990
V8i Auto (3.5) 5-door:	*International Off-Roader*, July 1993
V8i (3.9) 5-door:	*Autocar and Motor*, November 10, 1993
Mpi:	*Off Road and 4 Wheel Drive*, October 1993
	Land Rover Owner, October 1993
Tdi 3-door:	*Diesel Car*, May 1990
Tdi (200 Tdi) 5-door:	*Diesel Car*, December 1990
Tdi Auto 5-door:	*Diesel Car*, December 1993
Tdi ES 5-door:	*Diesel Car*, November 1994
Tdi ES Auto 5-dr:	*Autocar and Motor*, March 30,1994
Tdi (300 Tdi) 5-dr:	*International Off-Roader*, July 1994

There is also a book entitled *Land Rover Discovery: The Enthusiast's Companion*, written by the present author and published by Motor Racing Publications.

MAHINDRA JEEP

Background

The Mahindra CJ3 and CJ5 models are a breed apart in the 4x4 world. No other 4x4 so successfully captures the retro-look which became fashionable in many areas of the motor industry during the Nineties. However, the Mahindra was not styled deliberately to suit that fashion; its old-fashioned look comes from the fact that it is actually a licence-built and mechanically updated version of the CJ3B Jeep, which was introduced in 1953 and last built by Jeep in the USA as long ago as 1964.

The manufacturing licence is held by Mahindra and Mahindra of Bombay, but the vehicles sold in Britain are actually built up in Greece from kits exported from India. Most versions sold in the UK have a licence-built version of Peugeot's elderly 2.1-litre diesel engine, which was introduced back in 1968.

However, the Mahindra is not all old-fashioned. Its channel-section ladder-frame chassis with its leaf springs and drum brakes is mated to newer items like an (optional) overdrive gearbox, a brake servo, low-profile tyres and (since 1992) power-assisted steering. Similarly, Mahindra have developed their own long-wheelbase version of the CJ3, with 91 inches instead of 80 inches between the axle centres. Rather less common among the Mahindras in Britain today is a third model, the CJ5 which is an even longer-wheelbase model based on the Jeep of the same name built between 1955 and 1983. This can be fitted with a larger (2.5-litre) Peugeot diesel engine. Commercial versions have also been available.

The first Mahindras were sold in Britain in 1990. The original two companies which imported them collapsed, but the franchise now seems to be in more stable hands.

Vital statistics

Engine:	2,112cc indirect-injection diesel four-cylinder, with 60bhp at 4,200rpm and 89lb.ft at 2,000rpm or 2,498cc indirect-injection diesel four-cylinder, with 76bhp at 4,500rpm and 113lb.ft at 2,000rpm (CJ5 models only, 1991–1992)
Transmission:	Four-speed manual, with optional overdrive Selectable four-wheel drive with manually lockable freewheeling front hubs
Suspension:	Live axles front and rear; leaf springs all round
Steering:	Unassisted; power assistance option from 1992
Brakes:	Drums all round; standard power assistance

Dimensions:	Wheelbase	CJ3 SWB 80in (2,032mm)
		CJ3 LWB 91in (2,311mm)
		CJ5 96in (2,438mm)
	Length	CJ3 SWB 130in (3,302mm)
		CJ3 LWB 146in (3,708mm)
		CJ5 141in (3,581mm)
	Height	CJ3 72in (1,829mm)
		CJ5 76in (1,930mm)
	Width	CJ3 63in (1,600mm)
		CJ5 70in (1,778mm)
	Ground clearance	7.9in (200mm)
	Weight	CJ3 SWB 2,833lb (1,285kg)
		CJ3 LWB 2,943lb (1,335kg)
		CJ5 3,086lb (1,400kg)
Number of seats:	SWB 4	
	LWB 6	
Towing capacity:	3,300lb (1,500kg)	
Insurance rating:	Group 7	
Fuel consumption:	25–27mpg	
Top speed:	75mph	
0–60mph:	36sec	

Character summary

The Mahindra models are difficult to take seriously as everyday vehicles because of their many shortcomings: build quality, road performance and refinement are all way below the accepted norms. Nevertheless, they do make good weekend fun 4x4s as they offer open-air motoring, off-road ability and fashionable looks in a very reasonably priced package.

Performance summary

Acceleration in a Mahindra is leisurely, and top speed not really adequate for modern road conditions – certainly not on motorways. The steering offers little feel and the brakes are not very powerful; a harsh and bumpy ride is matched by high noise levels at all speeds.

Nevertheless, the Mahindras make good off-road performers. Short front and rear overhangs, and the short wheelbase (on CJ3 models) contribute to their ability in rough terrain. However, axle articulation is limited by the stiff leaf springs, and the standard wide low-profile tyres are present for looks rather than mud-plugging ability. The engine lacks bottom-end torque, but very low gearing compensates for this to a large extent.

Reliability, weaknesses, spares

The Mahindra models do not have a good reputation for a number of reasons. Build quality is almost invariably poor and many vehicles succumb to rust very early on. More recent examples have been rustproofed by the importers, although even that does not seem to prevent rust altogether. Water leaks into

Any resemblance between the 1993 Mahindra CJ3 and the famous American Jeep is far from coincidental because the Mahindra, assembled in Greece from kits imported from India, is built under licence and based on the Jeep CJ3B, which was last built in the USA in 1964.

This is the Mahindra CJ5, a longer-wheelbase vehicle based on the Jeep produced between 1955 and 1983; on this model a 2.5-litre Peugeot diesel engine is offered as an option to the 2.1-litre diesel fitted to all CJ3s. Power-assisted steering has been available since 1992.

the body are common, and the pre-1992 soft-tops do not last very long before tearing. Early models suffered from unreliable electrical components, although later ones seem to be better in this respect.

There can sometimes be long delays in obtaining spares, although the current importers claim to be able to provide most items within 48 hours of receiving an order.

Key specification changes in the UK

1990 (Jun): First imports

1991 (Jan): Limited Edition General Patton Special, based on standard-wheelbase CJ3

1991 (Jly): Standard models redesignated Classic; De Luxe versions introduced with rectangular headlamps, bull bar, alloy wheels, side steps, etc

1991 (Oct): CJ5 models introduced

1992 (Nov): Changed model-names (see below) under new importer; truck cab (commercial) versions of CJ5 discontinued; power-assisted steering and overdrive options introduced; improved soft-top, seats and heater

Nomenclature

Brave   1990–1992, short-wheelbase CJ3 models

Chief   1990–1992, long-wheelbase CJ3 models

De Luxe   1991–1992, Chief and Brave models with extra equipment and rectangular headlamps

General Patton   1991 Limited Edition with matt green paint, US Army star and serial numbers on bonnet, jerrycan, axe, shovel and hand-operated spotlight

Marksman   1991–1992, CJ5 models

MM 740   1992 on, CJ5 models

340 Classic   1992 on, short-wheelbase CJ3 models

340 Sport   1992 on, short-wheelbase CJ3 De Luxe models

540 Classic   1992 on, long-wheelbase CJ3 models

540 Sport   1992 on, long-wheelbase CJ3 De Luxe models

Resale values

The poor reputation acquired by early Mahindra imports has depressed resale values, the price-cuts made by the new importers in November 1992 doing nothing to prop them up. Although the vehicles are cheap to buy in the first place, depreciation is heavy.

Further reading

CJ3:   *Off Road and 4 Wheel Drive*, June 1993
            International Off-Roader, May 1995
            Off Road and 4 Wheel Drive, March 1994
            International Off-Roader, May 1994

MERCEDES-BENZ G-WAGEN

Background

The Mercedes-Benz G-Wagen almost certainly had its origins in the plan for a military Euro-Jeep in the mid-Seventies. When the Euro-Jeep failed to materialize, Mercedes decided to make use of the development effort they had put into the project and build a 4x4 anyway. They secured some military contracts in the late Seventies and then developed their new 4x4 as a civilian vehicle as well. It reached the market in 1979, but was not imported into the UK until 1981.

The G-Wagen (the name is short for Geländewagen, or Cross-Country Vehicle) never was an all-Mercedes product. It was developed jointly with the Austrian Steyr-Daimler-Puch concern and built at their factory in Graz. Mercedes' contribution was primarily drivetrains, plus interior design for the civilian versions. Part of the joint production deal was that Steyr should have sales rights in certain territories, so the vehicle wears Puch badges in some European countries and Steyr badges in Greece. There is even a Peugeot-

Although the Mercedes-Benz G-Wagen has been on sale in the UK since 1981 it has never sold in large numbers and only two estate models – this short-wheelbase three-door and a longer-wheelbase five-door version – have been imported. This 1990 model was offered with a choice of 2.3-litre four-cylinder and 2.8-litre six-cylinder petrol engines or a 3-litre indirect-injection diesel.

badged version with Peugeot running-gear, built under licence in France mainly for the French military.

G-Wagens come in two wheelbases and all variants are based upon a conventional ladder-frame chassis. Although a wide variety of body configurations is available overseas, the UK market has taken only the short-wheelbase three-door estates and long-wheelbase five-door estates. The three-door soft-top was briefly imported during 1983, but failed to find a market. Pre-1990 models are known as 460-series types and the facelifted models imported after 1990 are 463-series. The vehicle's chassis number will contain the relevant three-digit combination.

The G-Wagen has never sold as well as its makers predicted back in 1979 and sales have always been particularly poor in the UK (which is otherwise one of Mercedes' best export markets). Despite the excellent build quality associated with the marque, the vehicle's biggest problem is that it started life as a military-utility 4x4 and was pitchforked by its makers into the luxury off-roader market. So despite Mercedes' worthy efforts on the interior and on refinement levels, they were unable to make a silk purse out of a sow's ear. Although more luxurious and more powerful G-Wagen models have been available in Germany, the versions imported to the UK have always lacked the styling, convenience features and road performance which are necessary for success in the luxury 4x4 market.

Vital statistics

Engine:	2,299cc injected petrol four-cylinder, with 125bhp at 5,000rpm and 140lb.ft at 4,000rpm (1983–1990) or 2,746cc injected petrol six-cylinder, with 156bhp at 5,250rpm and 169lb.ft at 4,250rpm (1981–1990) or 2,962cc injected petrol six-cylinder, with 170bhp at 5,500rpm and 173lb.ft at 4,500rpm (1990 on) or 3,005cc indirect-injection five-cylinder diesel, with 88bhp at 4,000rpm and 127lb.ft at 2,400rpm (1981–1990) or 2,996cc indirect-injection six-cylinder diesel, with 113bhp at 4,600rpm and 141lb.ft at 2,700rpm (1990 on)
Transmission:	Four-speed (to 1986) or five-speed (from 1986) manual, or four-speed automatic (280GE and 300GE/G300 models) Selectable four-wheel drive (1981–1990) Permanent four-wheel drive with centre

In 1991 the G-Wagen was given a mild facelift incorporating a neater grille and auxiliary lights recessed into the front bumper and at the same time all models were equipped with permanent four-wheel drive. The power choice was between 3-litre six-cylinder petrol or diesel engines.

	differential lock (1990 on)	
	Front and rear differential locks optional	
	(1981–1986) or standard (1986 on)	
Suspension:	Live front and rear axles; coil springs all round; anti-roll bars on both axles	
Steering:	Power-assisted as standard	
Brakes:	Discs on the front wheels and drums on the rear; standard power assistance; ABS optional on early models and standard since 1990	
Dimensions:	Wheelbase	SWB 94.5in (2,400mm)
		LWB 112.2in (2,850mm)
	Length	SWB 164.7in (4,183mm)
		LWB 183.6in (4,663mm)
	Height	74.5in (1,892mm)
	Width	66.5in (1,690mm)
	Ground clearance	8.2in (208mm)
	Weight	230GE/G230 4,508lb (2,045kg)
		280GE SWB 4,288lb (1,945kg)
		280GE LWB 4,552lb (2,065kg)

Character summary

Mercedes-Benz products have traditionally been rather soulless models of efficiency, vehicles to be admired and respected rather than liked irrationally. The G-Wagen is no exception to this rule. It does everything expected of it without fuss, but equally without showing any quirks which would give it real character. In that context, its lack of road performance is an irritation.

Nevertheless, a G-Wagen makes a good, uncomplaining everyday vehicle, suitable for anything from hypermarket shopping to long-distance motorway cruising. For the latter, however, diesel models are best avoided. Long-wheelbase models are extremely spacious; short-wheelbase models have enough room behind the rear seats to fit two optional inward-facing seats.

Performance summary

Remarkably, Mercedes-Benz never saw fit to introduce turbodiesel versions of the G-Wagen to the UK market, even though turbodiesel engines were the

	300GE/G300 SWB 4,600lb (2,086kg) (2,270kg) 300GD/G300 Diesel SWB 4,600lb (2,086kg) 300GD/G300 Diesel LWB 4,900lb (2,222kg)
Number of seats:	SWB 5/7 LWB 5/9
Towing capacity:	SWB 5,780lb (2,620kg) LWB 6,500lb (2,950kg)
Insurance rating:	Group 12 (230GE/G230, 280GE, 300GD/G300 Diesel) Group 14 (300GE/G300)
Fuel consumption:	230GE/G230 11–21mpg 280GE 10–20mpg 300GE/G300 10–20mpg 300GD/G300 Diesel 14–24mpg
Top speed:	230GE/G230 95mph 280GE 94mph 300GE/G300 102mph 300GD/G300 Diesel 84mph
0–60mph:	230GE/G230 15.9sec 280GE 14.9sec 300GE/G300 12sec 300GD/G300 Diesel 25sec

norm for 4x4 estates and there were suitable engines available. This means that the diesel versions tend to be plodders, lacking in all sparkle: the later six-cylinder engine is better than the early five-cylinder, but its mid-range response is very disappointing. Petrol engines give unexciting performance, the later 3-litre type being the best.

The permanent four-wheel drive of the later 463-series model gives these better handling balance than early models and improves grip in the wet. Where available, automatic transmissions are preferable to the manuals, which have a heavy gearchange and similarly heavy clutch.

Reliability, weaknesses, spares

Like all Mercedes, the G-Wagen is extremely well-engineered, extremely reliable and extremely durable. Engines, for example, should give 150,000 miles without major trouble. However, build quality is not quite as good as on Mercedes saloons.

Mercedes parts are notoriously expensive, so it is fortunate that very little ever goes wrong with a G-Wagen. Service intervals are annoyingly frequent, but there are enough non-franchised Mercedes specialists in the UK for owners to make substantial savings over main dealer prices. Even so, no G-Wagen will ever be cheap to own.

Key specification changes in the UK

1981 (Oct):	460-Series LWB 280GE and 300GD estates introduced
1983 (Sep):	460-series SWB 230GE introduced; both Station Wagon and Soft Top models available
1985 (Oct):	Redesigned centre console and two-tone facia; central locking added to 230GE
1987 (Jan):	Differential locks standardized; five-speed manual gearboxes replaced four-speed; polyurethane wheelarch extensions added
1987 (Oct):	Rear number-plate relocated to the centre of split rear bumper; 230GE Soft Top discontinued
1991 (Jan):	463-Series facelift models introduced, with permanent four-wheel drive and deselectable ABS. Existing models replaced by 300GE and 300GD, both available as SWB or LWB
1992 (Oct):	Model names (and badges) changed to G300 and G300 Diesel; driver's airbag standardized

Nomenclature

Mercedes model-names are straightforward: the figure always reflects the engine size, so that a 230GE has a 2.3-litre engine, a 300GD has a 3-litre engine, and so on. The G in G-Wagen model names is self-explanatory. D stands for Diesel, and E for 'Einspritzung' (petrol injection).

In 1992, Mercedes changed their model-naming system by placing the type-letter ahead of the engine size code; thus, what had been a 300GE became a G300 and what had been a 300GD became a G300 Diesel.

The type-designations have never included an identifier for short-wheel-base or long-wheelbase.

Resale values
The relative unpopularity of the G-Wagen in the UK means that resale values have never been as strong as those of Mercedes cars. However, the vehicles tend to sell to owners or former owners of Mercedes products who expect to pay high prices for top-quality engineering; as a result, prices have never dropped disastrously. In the long term, gentle depreciation seems the most likely trend, but the limited number of potential buyers means that G-Wagens will sometimes be difficult to sell on.

Club information
There is a newly-formed club for G-Wagen owners. Contact the G-Wagen Owners' Association through:

Bill Jones
121 Goodshaw Lane
Rossendale
Lancashire BB4 8DJ
(Tel: 01706-227456)

Further reading
All models: *Off Road and 4 Wheel Drive*, August 1993
                   International Off-Roader, October 1994
230GE: *Off Road and 4 Wheel Drive*, July 1985
                   Motor, August 17, 1985
280GE: *Off Road and 4 Wheel Drive*, April 1986
300GD SWB 5-cyl: *Off Road and 4 Wheel Drive*, May 1985
                   Autocar and Motor, December 12, 1990
300GD SWB 6-cyl: *Diesel Car*, October 1991
300GD LWB 6-cyl: *Autocar and Motor*, February 6, 1991
300GE LWB: *International Off-Roader*, December 1993

MITSUBISHI SHOGUN
(first generation)

Background

Mitsubishi had built a version of the CJ Jeep under licence since the Fifties, but the Shogun was their first attempt at a dual-purpose off-roader. They designed both SWB and LWB versions, the SWB aimed at the weekend fun market and the LWB aimed at a market they had identified for a family estate car with 4x4 attributes at a price below that of the Range Rover. The Shogun (known as a Pajero in most overseas markets and as a Montero in the USA) was announced in Japan in 1982.

It came to Britain a year later, initially in SWB form only and initially wearing the Colt badges then used by its importer. The LWB models followed in 1984, and quickly hit the bullseye of their target market. The British importers reacted swiftly to customer preferences, fine-tuning the model mix to give maximum appeal, and by 1987 the LWB Shogun had become the definitive suburban 4x4. It was the best-selling family 4x4 of the Eighties, losing its crown only when the Land Rover Discovery appeared on the scene.

The Shogun always had a conventional ladder-frame chassis, but it broke new ground in the 4x4 world with its independent front suspension. This had twin wishbones and torsion bars, and gave ride and handling characteristics which were uncommonly good for a big 4x4 in the early to middle Eighties. It also had a chain-driven transfer box which ensured that transmission noise levels were low, and it pioneered automatic gearboxes with diesel engines in this area of the market.

The Shogun has few disadvantages. However, its unadventurously boxy styling has not dated well and is seen as a drawback by some buyers; also the high-roof LWB models available between 1985 and 1987 make the vehicle too tall for many multi-storey car parks and domestic garages.

The five-door Shogun turbodiesel entered the UK market in 1984 and was the best-selling family 4x4 until the arrival of the Land Rover Discovery.

Character summary

Despite an impressive track record in long-distance desert rallies like the Paris–Dakar, the Shogun's ruggedness takes second place to its docility and refinement. The LWB models are spacious and make extremely good towing vehicles: the Turbodiesel has won magazine awards for its towing ability in Britain. In general, they make excellent family transport. The SWB models

---

Vital statistics

Engine:	2,555cc caburettor petrol four-cylinder, with 103bhp at 4,500rpm and 142lb.ft at 2,500rpm (to March 1989) or 108bhp at 4,500rpm and 147lb.ft at 2,500rpm (from March 1989) or 2,346cc indirect-injection turbocharged diesel four-cylinder, with 84bhp at 4,200rpm and 133.5lb.ft at 2,000rpm or 2,477cc indirect-injection turbocharged diesel four-cylinder, with 84bhp at 4,200rpm and 140lb.ft at 2,000rpm or 2,477cc indirect-injection turbocharged and intercooled four-cylinder, with 94bhp at 4,200rpm and 173lb.ft at 2,000rpm or 2,972cc injected petrol V6, with 139bhp at 5000rpm and 166lb.ft at 3,000rpm
Transmission:	Five-speed manual; four-speed automatic option on LWB turbodiesel and V6 petrol models Selectable four-wheel drive with automatic freewheeling front hubs Limited-slip differential standard on V6 and part of Diamond Option Pack on others
Suspension:	Independent front suspension with wishbones, torsion bars and anti-roll bar Beam rear axle with semi-elliptic leaf springs or Beam rear axle with trailing arms, coil springs and anti-roll bar (1989 on)
Steering:	Power-assistance optional; standard on all LWB petrol V6 models and on all models from 1990
Brakes:	Disc brakes on the front wheels and drum brakes on the rear
Dimensions:	Wheelbase SWB 92.5in (2,305mm) LWB 106.1in (2,695mm)

have the usual problem of restricted luggage space in the rear.

All models of Shogun are well-finished, solid-feeling vehicles. Interior ambience is pleasant, but the neat dashboard appears busy, and the inclinometer and other instruments allegedly designed for off-road use are little more than gimmicks. Noise levels at speed can be quite high on all models except the petrol V6.

Length	SWB 155in (3,937mm)	
	LWB 181in (4,597mm)	
Height	73in (1,854mm) or	
	76in (1,930mm) with	
	high roof (LWB,	
	1985–87)	
Width	66in (1,676mm)	
Ground clearance	SWB 8.3in (210mm)	
	LWB 8.1in (205mm)	
Weight	SWB 3,240–3,560lb	
	(1,470–1,615kg),	
	depending on	
	model and	
	specification	
	LWB 3,748–4,012lb	
	(1,700–1,820kg),	
	depending on	
	model and	
	specification	
Number of seats:	SWB 5	
	LWB 7	
Towing capacity:	SWB 6,173lb (2,800kg)	
	LWB 7,275lb (3,300kg)	
Insurance rating:	Group 12	
Fuel consumption:	2.6 petrol	13–23mpg
	3.0 petrol	13–23mpg
	2.3 turbodiesel	23–33mpg
	2.5 turbodiesel	22–32mpg
Top speed:	2.6 petrol	90mph
	3.0 petrol	99mph
	2.3 turbodiesel	81mph
	2.5 turbodiesel	85mph
0–60mph:	2.6 petrol	10.9sec
	3.0 petrol	13.1sec
	2.3 turbodiesel	19.8sec
	2.5 turbodiesel	19sec

Performance summary

High performance never was the Shogun's strong suit, and the favourite turbodiesel models are only adequate in this respect, despite their strong mid-range acceleration; even the V6 petrol models are not really very fast. The vehicle's main attraction has always been that it feels much like a car to drive. The controls are light, the handling forgiving and the ride in the LWB models reasonable if rather firm. The final coil-sprung examples are best in the ride department; all SWB models have a rather more agitated ride than their LWB equivalents.

The main disadvantage is restricted rearward vision, caused by the externally-stowed spare wheel, the rear head restraints (which are removable) and by the stowage position of the rearmost seats on LWB models (although these can, of course, be lowered out of the way).

Off-road, the SWB Shogun is a very capable vehicle, despite the limitations of its independent front suspension. The LWB models are rather less impressive in the rough, mainly because of their longer wheelbases.

Reliability, weaknesses, spares

The biggest problem which afflicts early examples of the first-generation Shogun is rust. Rust protection was improved during 1986, but weak spots on early vehicles include the door bottoms, wheelarches and bonnet leading edge. Rust also tends to break out around holes where the bodywork has been drilled for accessories (such as lamp guards).

Interior trim is generally quite tough, but seat covers can sometimes split. Mechanical problems are uncommon. Engines are good for high mileages, but turbodiesels can crack cylinder heads (a problem usually betrayed by overheating). Turbochargers are normally reliable, but can wear if the recommended service oil changes are neglected. Gearboxes are robust in themselves, but often develop vibration and whine at high mileages.

Spares are readily available through the Mitsubishi dealer network. As with many Japanese vehicles, prices can be high: as so little goes wrong with the Shogun, few replacement parts are needed and consequently their cost cannot be kept down. There is no aftermarket support for Mitsubishi products in the UK.

Key specification changes in the UK

1983 (Jly):   SWB Estate and Soft Top models introduced, with 2.6-litre petrol engine
1984 (Jan):   2.3-litre turbodiesel option added
1984 (Oct):   LWB Estate introduced, with high-roof body and turbodiesel engine
1985 (Jan):   Soft Top discontinued
1985 (Mar):   LWB Estate available with 2.6-litre petrol engine
1986 (Oct):   LWB Estate available with low-roof body; 2.5-litre turbodiesel replaced 2.3-litre; automatic option introduced with turbodiesel engine; larger seats and better trim for all models

The 2.6-litre four-cylinder petrol-engined Shogun complete with optional bull bars. The boxy styling of first-generation vehicles, especially this short-wheelbase version, is accentuated by the Shogun's considerable body height.

1987 (Oct):   High-roof LWB Estate discontinued, leaving low-roof model available
1989 (Mar):   Intercooler added to turbodiesel engine; V6 engine introduced for LWB Estate; coil-spring rear suspension replaced leaf-spring type (initially on V6 model only); improved 5-speed gearbox for turbodiesel models; restyled trim for SWB models
1991 (May):   All models replaced by second-generation Shogun

Nomenclature
Diamond Option Pack   Includes limited-slip differential in rear axle, electric windows, etc

Resale values
Despite the introduction in 1991 of replacement models, the first-generation Shoguns have retained firm resale values. The best bets are long-wheelbase family estates, particularly with the turbodiesel and V6 petrol engines. Values will probably remain quite firm until large quantities of the newer models are available on the used vehicle market.

Further reading
All models: *Off Road and 4 Wheel Drive*, August 1991
                            Off Road and 4 Wheel Drive, July 1993
                            International Off-Roader, February 1995
SWB 2.6 petrol: *Off Road and 4 Wheel Drive*, Spring 1984
SWB 2.3 turbodiesel: *Off Road and 4 Wheel Drive*, July 1986
SWB 2.5 turbodiesel: *Diesel Car*, December 1988
LWB 2.6 petrol: *Off Road and 4 Wheel Drive*, August 1985
LWB 2.3 turbodiesel: *Off Road and 4 Wheel Drive*, March 1985
LWB 2.5 turbodiesel: *Autocar*, June 17, 1987
                            Diesel Car, December 1988

MITSUBISHI SHOGUN
(second generation)

Background

The second-generation Shogun which was introduced in 1991 was a very clever piece of product development. It retained all the strengths of its predecessors, but dressed them up in more aerodynamic and contemporary styling and added improved equipment levels. The package allowed the range to be moved further upmarket in many territories, including the UK, yet without losing the market base on which it had built its reputation. With the arrival in 1994 of the top-specification 3.5-litre V6 models, the Shogun moved into direct competition with the Toyota Land Cruiser VX and the Range Rover in the luxury 4x4 market, while the cheaper models remained competitive in the family estate market where the first-generation Shoguns had been so successful.

However, there is a far greater variety of Shogun models available worldwide than appears in British showrooms, and in most territories the vehicle has retained the Pajero name. The full model range includes variants such as a high-roof LWB estate and a SWB cabriolet, and of course equipment levels vary from country to country. So it was that the British importers were quickly able to bring in cheaper models at the beginning of 1995 when the market seemed to demand it. The importers claim that the Shogun would sell even more strongly in the UK if sales were not limited to around 3,600 examples a year by the import quota agreement.

All Shoguns were upgraded at the beginning of 1994, with both mechanical and cosmetic improvements.

The Mitsubishi Shogun five-door with the latest 2.8-litre four-cylinder turbodiesel engine and five-spoke alloy wheels introduced in 1994.

Character summary

The Shogun is a deliberately stylish 4x4, with an aggressive appearance on top models as a result of its wide wheelarches. These are absent from base-model LWB examples. The styling translates less successfully into SWB form, and the three-door models tend to look rather dumpy and foreshortened.

High equipment levels on top models and very comfortable seats right across the range make these very good road vehicles. The LWB estates have light and spacious interiors and are ideally suited as family vehicles; they also make excellent tow cars. However, they do feel rather large and cumbersome, even when fitted with the full complement of driving aids including automatic transmission and power-assisted steering.

Vital statistics

Engine:	2,972cc petrol V6, with 178bhp at 5,500rpm and 188lb.ft at 4,000rpm or 3,497cc petrol V6, with 205bhp at 5,000rpm and 221lb.ft at 3,000rpm (1994 on) or 2,477cc indirect-injection intercooled turbodiesel four-cylinder, with 98bhp at 4,200rpm and 177lb.ft at 2,000rpm (LWB models from 1991–1994 and all SWB models) or 2,835cc indirect-injection intercooled turbodiesel four-cylinder, with 123bhp at 4,000rpm and 215lb.ft at 2,000rpm (LWB models only, from 1994)
Transmission:	Five-speed manual; four-speed automatic option (V6 only 1991–1993, LWB turbodiesels as well from 1994) Selectable four-wheel drive Freewheeling front hubs Automatic locking centre differential and manually lockable rear differential
Suspension:	Independent front suspension with wishbones, torsion bar springs and anti-roll bar; live rear axle with three links and coil springs
Steering:	Power-assisted as standard
Brakes:	Ventilated discs at the front, solid discs at the rear; power-assisted as standard ABS on 3.5-litre V6 models, optional on others
Dimensions:	Wheelbase SWB 95.3in (2,420mm) LWB 107.3in (2,725mm) Length SWB 163in (4,140mm) LWB 186in (4,725mm)

Performance summary

The second-generation Shoguns continue the tradition established by their predecessors of being easy to drive. The V6 petrol engines give very good road performance, and the 3.5-litre V6 (also seen in the Mitsubishi 3000GT sports coupé) is a particularly smooth, refined and powerful unit. The later 2.8-litre turbodiesel is also an excellent engine, though it naturally lacks the sparkle of the big petrol engines.

On the road, these vehicles feel very stable, with good cornering abilities. The complicated Super Select transmission takes some time to understand, but presents no actual difficulties (it allows four-wheel drive to be selected on the move and automatically locks the centre differential if wheelspin threatens; the rear differential can be locked separately). As with earlier Shoguns, rearward visibility is poor if the occasional seats are in their stowed positions.

Off-road, a lack of wheel articulation at the front is the Shogun's biggest failing. The SWB models are, of course, more able than the LWB estates. The V6 petrol engines are biased towards road use and are not over-endowed with bottom-end torque although they are perfectly adequate for most situations. The 2.8-litre turbodiesel, on the other hand, is an excellent engine for off-road use.

Height	72in (1,828mm)
Width	70in (1,778mm)
Ground clearance	SWB turbodiesel 8.9in (225mm)
	SWB petrol and all LWB 8.5in (215mm)
Weight	SWB 3.0 petrol 3,880lb (1,760kg)
	SWB 3.0 auto 3,902lb (1,770kg)
	SWB 3.5 petrol 3,990lb (1,810kg)
	SWB turbodiesel 3,870lb (1,755kg)
	LWB 3.0 petrol 4,299lb (1,950kg)
	LWB 3.5 petrol 4,387lb (1,990kg)
	LWB turbodiesel 4,497lb (2,040kg)
	LWB turbodiesel auto 4,508lb (2,045kg)
Number of seats:	SWB 4/5
	LWB 5/7

Early second-generation three-door and five-door Shoguns, which were introduced in 1991 with a choice of 3.6-litre V6 petrol or 2.5-litre four-cylinder turbodiesel engines.

Reliability, weaknesses, spares

The second-generation Shoguns are built to an impressively high standard and have so far shown up no serious weaknesses. Spares are available only through Mitsubishi dealers and can be rather expensive. A wide range of accessories can be bought through dealerships.

Towing capacity:	SWB 6,173lb (2,200kg)	
	LWB 7,275lb (3,300kg)	
Insurance rating:	Group 13	
Fuel consumption:	SWB 3.0 petrol	20mpg
	SWB 3.5 petrol	18.3mpg
	SWB turbodiesel	24mpg
	LWB 3.0 petrol	20mpg
	LWB 3.5 petrol	18.3mpg
	LWB turbodiesel	23mpg
Top speed:	SWB 3.0 petrol	103mph (Auto 100mph)
	SWB 3.5 petrol	116mph
	SWB turbodiesel	91mph
	LWB 3.0 petrol	103mph (Auto 100mph)
	LWB 3.5 petrol	116mph
	LWB 2.5 turbodiesel	88mph
	LWB 2.8 turbodiesel	94mph
0–60mph:	SWB 3.0 petrol	13.2sec
	SWB 3.5 petrol	10.7sec
	SWB turbodiesel	20sec
	LWB 3.0 petrol	13.2sec
	LWB 3.5 petrol	10.7sec
	LWB turbodiesel	17.1sec

Key specification changes in the UK

1991 (May): Range introduced to UK, with 3-litre petrol V6 and 2.5-litre turbodiesel engines

1994 (Feb): 3.5-litre petrol V6 and 2.8-litre turbodiesel engines introduced; 2.5-litre turbodiesel dropped from LWB models; automatic transmission available for LWB turbodiesels; stronger five-speed gearbox; redesigned alloy wheels

1995 (Jan): Base-specification GLX SWB and LWB models added to range

Nomenclature

Diamond Option Pack   Includes ABS, variable-rate dampers, electronic compass and thermometer; LWB models also have leather upholstery and heated front seats

GLS   High-line turbodiesel SWB and LWB (1995 on)

GLX   Base-model turbodiesel SWB and LWB (1995 on)

Resale values

The second-generation Shoguns – LWB models in particular – are widely liked, and used examples do not linger long in the showrooms. Resale values are firm and will probably continue to be so for several more years.

Further reading

SWB 3000 V6:   *International Off-Roader*, February 1994

LWB 3000 V6:   *Autocar and Motor*, June 20,1991

SWB 2500 turbodiesel: *Diesel Car*, February 1992

LWB 2500 turbodiesel: *Diesel Car*, December 1992

LWB 2800 turbodiesel Auto: *Off Road and 4 Wheel Drive*, July 1994

More basic GLX-specification Shoguns were added to the range at the beginning of 1995 in both short-wheelbase and long-wheelbase forms.

NISSAN PATROL
(first generation)

Background

The MQ model Nissan Patrol which was introduced to the UK in 1982 was the first model of Patrol to be imported; to UK buyers it therefore qualifies as the first-generation Patrol. However, the very first Patrol appeared as long ago as 1951 and was a very different sort of vehicle, for like so many light four-wheel drives of the period, it was based heavily on the war-time Jeep.

By the time the MQ models were announced in Japan towards the end of 1981, the Patrol had evolved into a rugged vehicle, particularly suitable for the dirt roads of Africa and South-East Asia. It had no pretensions to sophistication: the Patrol was purely a workhorse. Nevertheless, the UK importers (then using the Datsun name) believed that there was room for the vehicle in the burgeoning four-wheel drive market. So, from January 1982 they began to import both SWB and LWB types.

The Patrol was distinguished from many of its rivals by the fact that both SWB and LWB variants were powered by six-cylinder engines, originally designed for some of Nissan's light commercials. However, its unsophisticated nature meant that it was never a strong seller in the UK four-wheel drive market, being outsold by rivals from Toyota and Isuzu in particular. Probably fewer than 7,000 were sold between 1982 and the end of imports in 1993.

The first examples were imported from Japan, but after January 1983 all Patrols for the UK market were built at Nissan's Motor Iberica plant in Spain. As usual, the Patrol was available in a very wide range of models, but the UK importers saw fit to import only two types, these being a two-door Hard Top and a four-door Estate.

The Patrol continues in production in Spain for various military and commercial markets.

The Nissan Patrol estate, introduced to the UK market in 1982, was unusual in that both its petrol and its diesel engines were six-cylinder units.

105

Character summary

The Patrol is a tremendously rugged vehicle, which scores with its reliability and simplicity. To consider it alongside stylish and sophisticated urban four-wheel drives is to do it an injustice: it was simply never intended to compete in the same market. The LWB models in particular have a truck-like character which has its own appeal, and they make excellent towing vehicles. However, they are best considered as alternatives to leaf-sprung Land Rovers rather than as contenders in the family estate market. SWB models are tough but lack the

---

Vital statistics

Engine:	2,753cc carburettor petrol six-cylinder, with 120bhp at 4,800rpm and 149lb.ft at 3,200rpm (1982–1989)
	or 2,962cc carburettor petrol six-cylinder, with 135bhp at 4,800rpm and 165lb.ft at 3,000rpm (1989 on)
	or 3,246cc diesel six-cylinder, with 95bhp at 3,600rpm and 160lb.ft at 1,800rpm (1982–1989)
	or 2,826cc diesel six-cylinder, with 92bhp at 4,800rpm and 127lb.ft at 2,400rpm (1989 on)
	or 2,826cc turbocharged diesel six-cylinder, with 114bhp at 4,400rpm and 176lb.ft at 2,400rpm (1989–1992), uprated to 117bhp (1992–1993)
Transmission:	Four-speed manual (to 1986); five-speed manual (1986 on)
	Selectable four-wheel drive
	Manually lockable freewheeling front hubs (to 1986); automatic freewheeling front hubs (1986 on)
	Limited-slip differential in the rear axle (petrol models, 1989 on)
Suspension:	Live front and rear axles; semi-elliptic leaf springs all round; front anti-roll bar
Steering:	Power-assisted as standard
Brakes:	Discs on the front wheels, drums on the rear; standard power assistance

Dimensions:		
	Wheelbase	SWB 92.5in (2,350mm)
		LWB 118.1in (3,000mm)
	Length	SWB 160in (4,070mm)
		LWB 186in (4,725mm)

sparkle so often appreciated in the weekend fun vehicle market.

Before 1989, interior trim was rather basic and reminiscent of commercial vehicles rather than passenger-carrying types. The revised models introduced in 1989 had much more appealing interiors, although these are still quite basic. Body panels feel and look flimsy, and the slab-sided styling is unappealing to many buyers. A further drawback is the deep tailgate, which makes loading awkward. Nevertheless, the load area of the LWB models is cavernous.

Height	SWB 72.6in (1,845mm)	
	LWB 71in (1,805mm)	
Width	SWB 66.5in (1,690mm)	
	LWB 66.5in (1,690mm)	
Ground clearance	SWB 8.5in (215mm)	
	LWB 7.5in (190mm)	
Weight	SWB petrol 3,758lb (1,705kg)	
	SWB diesel 4,155lb (1,885kg)	
	LWB petrol 4,034lb (1,830kg)	
	LWB diesel 4,431lb (2,010kg)	
Number of seats:	SWB 4/5	
	LWB 5/7	
Towing capacity:	SWB 7,716lb (3,500kg)	
	LWB 7,716lb (3,500kg)	
Insurance rating:	2.8 petrol	Group 9
	2.8 diesel	Group 9
	2.8 turbodiesel	Group 10
	3.2 diesel	Group 10
	3.0 petrol	Group 10
Fuel consumption:	2.8 petrol	11–21mpg
	3.0 petrol	16–26mpg
	2.8 turbodiesel	18–30mpg
	3.2 diesel	18–28mpg
Top speed:	2.8 petrol	85mph
	3.0 petrol	101mph
	2.8 turbodiesel	90mph
	3.2 diesel	84mph
0–60mph:	2.8 petrol	16.8sec
	3.0 petrol	16.3sec
	2.8 turbodiesel	21.6sec
	3.2 diesel	22.1sec

The short-wheelbase hardtop version of the first UK-market Nissan Patrols, which from 1983 onwards were manufactured at Nissan's plant in Spain.

Performance summary

The biggest fault of the early Patrols is their uncompromisingly firm ride; the softer road springs fitted to post-1990 models make a worthwhile difference in this area. Gearboxes on vehicles of all ages can also be baulky when cold.

Much depends on the engine fitted to the Patrol. The early 3.2-litre diesel has plenty of low-down torque but constantly reminds the driver of its light-truck origins; the later 2.8-litre diesel is much more refined and free-revving, and in turbocharged form provides reasonable acceleration and fairly quiet cruising at motorway speeds. The petrol engines offer modest acceleration for their size, but nothing like the performance available from engines of comparable capacity in other four-wheel drives.

On the road, the SWB vehicles present no problems, but the LWB models always feel big and a trifle cumbersome, despite the standard power-assisted steering. Brakes are strong and reassuring on all models. Off the road, the SWB is not as good as its specification suggests it might be, while the immense wheelbase of the LWB models can make them rather a handful in the rough. Axle articulation is good for a leaf-sprung design, but the departure angle is limited by the spare-wheel stowage position under the long rear overhang.

Reliability, weaknesses, spares

Whatever their other limitations may be, the MQ Patrols are certainly reliable. All engines offered in the range are capable of very high mileages without major overhaul – up to 200,000 miles in many cases. Nevertheless, overheating and blown head gaskets seem to be quite common.

While the chassis is rarely affected by serious rust, the bottom half of the tailgate can corrode badly, especially around the hinges. Heavy off-road use causes wear in the front leaf spring hanger bolts, which is revealed by a clonk as the steering wheel is turned.

The biggest disadvantage in the UK is that relatively few of these vehicles were sold and that even Nissan dealers are often unfamiliar with them. Many dealers keep very few Patrol parts in stock and there can be long waits before spares ordered specially become available.

Key specification changes in the UK

1982 (Jan): Range announced with round headlamps, vinyl seats in SWB and cloth in LWB, four-speed gearbox and 2.8-litre petrol or 3.2-litre diesel engines; Datsun badges

1984 (Mar): Revised front with new grille and rectangular headlamps; white spoked steel wheels; colour-matched facia; Nissan badges

1986 (Sep): Five-speed gearbox standardized

1989 (Sep): Revised grille and indicators; body-colour wheelarch extensions; 3-litre petrol engine replaced 2.8-litre and 2.8-litre turbodiesel replaced 3.2-litre diesel; 2.8-litre naturally-aspirated diesel introduced; limited-slip rear differential for petrol models

1992 (Jan): All models temporarily unavailable

1992 (Mar): All models available again

1992 (Apr): Range supplemented by Patrol GR models

1993 (Jly): Imports discontinued

Resale values

Resale values of these Patrols have remained surprisingly strong in view of the limited market, which must be a tribute to their durability. However, early vehicles can now be bought quite cheaply, and it can only be a matter of time before prices of the later types begin to fall steeply. It is probably the relative scarcity of used second-generation Patrols on the UK market which is keeping prices at their present levels.

Nevertheless, a used Patrol can sometimes be quite hard to sell on. Petrol models are rare and not much liked, most buyers preferring the big diesels. The post-1990 models with their improved specifications and better engines are the most desirable of all, but they are not numerous. Bull bars and other accessories enhance the Patrol's rather plain appearance and can improve the chances of reselling a vehicle.

Further reading

All models: *Off Road and 4 Wheel Drive*, October 1992
                        International Off-Roader, July 1993
                        Off Road and 4 Wheel Drive, November 1993
SWB 3.2 diesel: *Off Road and 4 Wheel Drive*, September 1986
LWB 2.8 turbodiesel: *Off Road and 4 Wheel Drive*, July 1991

NISSAN PATROL
(second generation)

Background
The second-generation Patrol was introduced in Japan during 1989, but was not imported into Britain by Nissan until 1992. By that date, several examples had already been imported privately and as a result there are some examples around with specifications which differ from the one eventually adopted for the UK; among them are examples of the ungainly-looking High Roof Station Wagon.

The Patrol GR (as it is more properly called) came with a very different image from its predecessors. Where they were unashamedly truck-like, the GR could be bought with a wide range of extra equipment and had pretensions to the family and even the luxury estate markets. Nevertheless, it remained a fundamentally rugged vehicle. In some respects it is rather less different from the first-generation Patrol than it initially appears: many body panels, for example, are shared between the two vehicles.

UK sales have so far been much stronger than those of the old-model Patrols, but the Patrol GR is still far from being a bestseller.

The second-generation Nissan Patrol, known as the GR, was imported into the UK from 1992 and although as rugged as its predecessor was offered with a much wider choice of optional equipment in order to widen its appeal to the family user.

Vital statistics

Engine:	4,169cc injected petrol six-cylinder, with 167bhp at 4,000rpm and 236lb.ft at 3,200rpm (LWB models only) or 4,169cc diesel six-cylinder, with 124bhp at 4,000rpm and 201lb.ft at 2,000rpm
Transmission:	Five-speed manual; four-speed automatic option with petrol engine only Selectable four-wheel drive; Automatic freewheeling front hubs Rear differential lock
Suspension:	Live axles front and rear; coil springs all round
Steering:	Power-assisted as standard
Brakes:	Ventilated discs all round, with standard power assistance

Dimensions:

Wheelbase	SWB 94.5in (2,400mm)	
	LWB 116.9in (2,970mm)	
Length	SWB 171.9in (4,368mm)	
	LWB 195in (4,953mm)	
Height	71in (1,803mm)	
Width	76in (1,930mm)	
Ground clearance	SWB 8.7in (221mm)	
	LWB 8.5in (216mm)	
Weight	SWB diesel	4,564lb (2,070kg)
	LWB petrol	4,663lb (2,115kg)
	LWB diesel	4,917lb (2,230kg)

Number of seats:	SWB 4/5	
	LWB 5/7	
Towing capacity:	7,700lb (3,500kg)	
Insurance rating:	Group 12	
Fuel consumption:	SWB diesel	22.1mpg
	LWB petrol	17.6mpg
	LWB diesel	20.7mpg
Top speed:	SWB diesel	90mph
	LWB petrol	103mph
	LWB diesel	86mph
0–60mph:	SWB diesel	15.7sec
	LWB petrol	14.3sec
	LWB diesel	20.7sec

Character summary

The Nissan Patrol GR has plenty of aggressive presence, although its styling could hardly be called attractive. Basically slab-sided like the first-generation Patrol, it nevertheless has flared wheelarches and a wider track to give it a subtly different stance. In LWB form, the vehicle excels as a spacious seven-seater family estate, although it is not actually as big inside as its appearance suggests: in fact, the interior is rather narrow compared with the overall width of the vehicle.

The Patrol GR is also rather less sophisticated than its image would suggest. Details such as the dated-looking dashboard give away that this Patrol was intended just as much as its predecessors for markets where ruggedness matters more than style. Three-door SWB models are less well-equipped than the LWB five-doors, which include air conditioning as part of their standard specification. The twin unequal-sized rear doors make loading much easier than in the earlier models with their drop-down tailgates, and the stowage space behind the rear seats in SWB models is much larger than average.

Performance summary

The big 4.2-litre six-cylinder diesel is a quite remarkable engine, offering huge pulling power and unusual refinement, even though outright power is not up with the class leaders. The petrol engine has a very different character and is quite lively, although it is still fundamentally a lazy engine and the sheer weight of the LWB models for which it is available prevents performance from having too much sparkle.

On the road, these Patrols give a comfortable ride and are impressively stable vehicles with predictable cornering behaviour despite a constant impression of nose-heaviness. However, their steering feels vague and lifeless at speed, and the gearshift on manual-transmission examples is not up to the refined pretensions of the rest of the vehicle.

Off the road, the coil-spring suspension gives plenty of axle articulation and low-down torque from the diesel engine makes the SWB models excellent performers. SWB Patrols also have larger (16-inch) wheels than the LWB types, which further adds to their off-road ability. On manual models, the synchromesh fitted to reverse gear allows a driver to rock the vehicle back and forth easily to help gain traction when bogged down.

Reliability, weaknesses, spares

In the short time since the Patrol GR models went on sale in the UK, there has been nothing to suggest anything other than exemplary reliability. Nor have any consistent weaknesses shown up. The model appears to be very much better supported by Nissan dealers than its predecessors, although as before there is no aftermarket support.

Key specification changes in the UK

1992 (Apr):   LWB petrol models introduced to UK in SLX form; automatic transmission optional

The Patrol GR in five-door SGX and three-door SLX forms; automatic transmission is standard on the 4.2-litre petrol-engined SGX models, as are leather upholstery and the three-spoke alloy wheels.

1993 (Jan):   SWB models and LWB diesels introduced; SGX version of LWB petrol announced, with automatic transmission as standard
1993 (Oct):   LWB petrol SLX model discontinued; heated front seats for remaining LWB models; minor interior changes for all models

Nomenclature
SGX   High-line models, with leather upholstery, chrome bumpers and mirrors, three-spoke alloy wheels, etc
SLX   Base models, with cloth upholstery and painted bumpers and mirrors

Resale values
Depreciation on these models is average, despite their excellent reputation. One reason why resale values are not stronger must be the rather lack-lustre image of the older Patrols, which will undoubtedly cling to the GR models for some time to come.

Further reading
SWB diesel: *Off Road and 4 Wheel Drive*, June 1993
                         International Off-Roader, March 1994
LWB petrol, manual: *International Off-Roader*, April 1992
                         Off Road and 4 Wheel Drive, July 1992
                         International Off-Roader, October 1992
LWB petrol, auto: *Off Road and 4 Wheel Drive*, May 1993

NISSAN TERRANO II

Background

Nissan's track record in building four-wheel drive vehicles was already good before the company linked up with Ford to build what became the Terrano II when badged as a Nissan or the Maverick when badged as a Ford. The original Nissan Terrano was a quite different vehicle, being essentially a LWB estate-bodied derivative of a Nissan pick-up (not unlike the Toyota 4-Runner in concept), which was also known as a Pathfinder in some markets.

The Terrano II was designed to complement the old Terrano and to give Nissan a contender in the smart, weekend fun three-door 4x4 market where its SWB Patrol was proving too basic to attract some customers. It was also designed to be much more car-like than other Nissan four-wheel drives. In Nissan's marketing phrase, the new Terrano was an "all-roader".

In all important respects, the Nissan Terrano II is identical to the Ford Maverick. A different grille, bumper and spoiler assembly at the front is complemented by appropriate badges; wheels differ and the interior trim materials are different. In the UK, direct clashes are prevented by a careful choice of models, and none of the three versions of the Terrano clashes directly with the Ford models sold in the same market. In other countries, other versions of the Terrano (and of the Ford) are available.

As far as the UK market is concerned, the Terrano comes in both SWB and LWB forms, both with estate-type bodies. Engines are either petrol or turbodiesel and are exactly the same as those in the Maverick, both being of Nissan origin. The Terrano models do not include a petrol-engined SWB, and fit neatly between the base-level and high-line Mavericks. Indications so far are that the Terrano is selling in roughly half the numbers of the Maverick.

All Terranos are built on the same Spanish production lines as their Maverick counterparts.

The LX version of the three-door Terrano II, which is only available with a 2.7-litre four-cylinder turbodiesel engine, bridges the gap between the two specifications offered with the almost identical Ford Maverick.

Vital statistics

Engine:	2,389cc injected petrol four-cylinder, with 122bhp at 5,200rpm and 146lb.ft at 2,200rpm (LWB models only) or 2,663cc indirect-injection turbodiesel four-cylinder, with 99bhp at 4,000rpm and 164lb.ft at 2,200rpm
Transmission:	Five-speed manual Selectable four-wheel drive Automatic freewheeling front hubs Limited-slip differential in rear axle
Suspension:	Independent front suspension, with twin wishbones and torsion bar springs; live rear axle with coil springs
Steering:	Power-assisted as standard on all models
Brakes:	Ventilated discs at the front and drums at the rear, with standard power assistance

Dimensions:

Wheelbase	SWB	96.4in (2,450mm)
	LWB	104.3in (2,650mm)
Length	SWB	162in (4,115mm)
	LWB	181in (4,597mm)
Height		71in (1,803mm)
Width		68in (1,727mm)
Ground clearance	SWB	8.5in (216mm)
	LWB	8.3in (211mm)
Weight	SWB diesel	3,811lb (1,729kg)
	LWB petrol	3,855lb (1,749kg)
	LWB diesel	4,075lb (1,848kg)

Number of seats:	SWB	4/5
	LWB	7
Towing capacity:	SWB	5,070lb (2,300kg)
	LWB	5,687lb (2,580kg)
Insurance rating:	Group 10	
Fuel consumption:	Petrol models	23.1mpg
	Turbodiesel models	25.9mpg
Top speed:	SWB turbodiesel	85mph
	LWB petrol	100mph
	LWB turbodiesel	85mph
0–60mph:	SWB turbodiesel	23.6sec
	LWB petrol	14.2sec
	LWB turbodiesel	23.6sec

The five-door Terrano II in its more luxurious SLX trim is instantly recognizable by its three-spoke alloy wheels, although the bull bar is optional.

Character summary

The SWB Terrano is a curious hybrid of hot hatch and four-wheel drive machine; despite credible off-road performance, it was very clearly designed to make former car drivers feel at home in their new surroundings. Although interior stowage space for oddments is good, the SWB has the familiar problem of inadequate luggage room behind the rear seats.

The LWB Terrano has the same car-like feel to it and makes a good family estate. However, the occasional seats in the rear are not very comfortable, and the vehicle is best considered as a five-seater with only occasional seven-seat capacity.

Both SWB and LWB Terranos have a rather insubstantial feel to them, and this again makes them feel more like cars than like traditionally rugged four-wheel drives.

Performance summary

The SWB Terrano comes only with the turbodiesel engine in the UK, which gives it adequate but not particularly inspiring road performance. However, both this and the turbodiesel LWB make good motorway cruisers. The petrol-engined LWB offers better acceleration and a higher top speed in return for considerably heavier fuel consumption.

All models are very easy to drive, with car-like handling and responses. However, the SWB can feel twitchy in corners, and it pitches and bounces more than the smooth-riding LWB.

Off-road, the Terrano is surprisingly able. The greater length of the LWB models obviously makes them rather less agile than the SWB types and the turbodiesel engine is surprisingly lacking in off-boost bottom-end torque. However, all varieties of Terrano are perfectly capable of the tasks likely to be thrown at them in occasional recreational off-roading.

Reliability, weaknesses, spares

The Terrano is too new at present for any realistic evaluation of its reliability or long-term weaknesses. However, the good reliability record of previous Nissan four-wheel drives suggests that serious problems are unlikely to develop. Spares are available through the large Nissan dealership network; there is, however, no aftermarket.

Key specification changes in the UK

1993 (Jly):   Range introduced to UK

Nomenclature

LX   Base models
SLX   High-line models

Resale values

Relatively few Terrano IIs have filtered down through the secondhand market yet, so it is therefore difficult to say whether resale values are holding up. However, there is no reason to suppose that values will be anything other than firm for the next few years.

Further reading

SWB turbodiesel: *Off Road and 4 Wheel Drive*, October 1993
LWB petrol: *Off Road and 4 Wheel Drive*, November 1993
    International Off-Roader, February 1995
LWB turbodiesel SLX: *Diesel Car*, March 1994

The three-door model, seen here in SLX trim and powered by the turbodiesel engine, was the first of the Terrano IIs to enter the UK market in 1993. Off-road performance is generally considered to be excellent.

RANGE ROVER
(first generation four-door models)

Background

The Range Rover was the vehicle which really started the 4x4 estate boom outside the USA. It was designed in the mid-Sixties to meet the growing demand for a light 4x4 which was capable of rough-terrain work in pursuit of leisure activities, towing a caravan or boat, and doubling as fast road transport. It took one stage further the concept which some American 4x4s had pioneered in the first half of the Sixties and was announced to an ecstatic reaction in 1970. Although Land Rover announced the second-generation Range Rover during 1994, the original vehicle remained in production to see out its quarter-century anniversary in 1995.

The Range Rover was successful because it was a genuine dual-purpose vehicle, rugged and able enough to be used in demanding off-road situations and yet sufficiently stylish, fast and roadable to be used as an ordinary road car. Over the years, it became a status symbol as buyers demanded more and more creature comforts, and the showroom price escalated. Towards the end of the Seventies, it was the Range Rover's success which prompted Japanese makers to develop cheaper imitations such as the Mitsubishi Shogun and Isuzu Trooper.

For the first 11 years of its life, the Range Rover was available only as a two-door vehicle with a horizontally split tailgate. Demand forced its manufacturers to introduce a four-door body in 1981 (there had been a limited number of conversions before then), and thereafter almost all Range Rovers had four doors: two-door models disappeared from the UK market in 1986, although there was a special-edition two-door model in 1990. From

Demand for a four/five-door Range Rover was finally satisfied with the introduction of this model in 1981, 11 years after the launch of the original two/three-door vehicle. It was an instant success.

Vital statistics

Engine: 3,528cc carburettor petrol V8, with 125bhp at 4,000rpm and 190lb.ft at 2,500rpm (1981–1985)
or 3,528cc carburettor petrol V8, with 127bhp at 4,000rpm and 194lb.ft at 2,500rpm (1985–1986, base models)
or 3,528cc injected petrol V8, with 165bhp at 4,000rpm and 206lb.ft at 3,200rpm (1985–1986 Vogue; all models, 1986–1989)
or 3,947cc injected petrol V8, with 185bhp at 4,750rpm and 235lb.ft at 2,600rpm (1989–1992)
or 3,947cc injected petrol V8, with 181bhp at 4,750rpm and 231lb.ft at 3,100rpm (1992 on)
or 4,278cc injected petrol V8, with 200bhp at 4,850rpm and 250lb.ft at 3,250rpm (Vogue LSE models)
or 2,393cc turbocharged and intercooled indirect-injection diesel four-cylinder, with 112bhp at 4,200rpm and 183lb.ft at 2,400rpm (1986–1989)
or 2,500cc turbocharged and intercooled indirect-injection diesel four-cylinder, with 119bhp at 4,200rpm and 209lb.ft at 1,950rpm (1989–1992)
or 2,495cc turbocharged and intercooled direct-injection diesel four-cylinder, with 111bhp at 4,000rpm and 195lb.ft at 1,800rpm (1992 on)

Transmission: Four-speed manual (to 1983) or five-speed manual (1983 on; improved in 1994); or three-speed automatic (1982–1985) or four-speed automatic (1985 on)
Permanent four-wheel drive with lockable centre differential or (1988 on) automatic locking centre differential

Suspension: Live front and rear axles; coil springs all round, except Vogue SE and Vogue LSE from 1992 with air springs. Air springs optional on other models, 1992 on. Front axle has radius arms and a Panhard rod; rear axle has radius arms and an A-frame with self-levelling strut (no self-

1992, a long-wheelbase model (the Vogue LSE) was added to the range and offered additional legroom in the rear; air suspension came as standard on this and on the contemporary top-model standard-wheelbase Vogue SE. The two-door models are now generally disregarded by all except enthusiast buyers, and this survey covers four-door models only. In practice, few base-model four-doors were sold in the UK after 1984, the the majority of vehicles having the luxurious Vogue specification or higher.

Character summary
The Range Rover has an almost unique ability to convey a sense of well-being to driver and passengers; in that respect, its familiar appellation of the Rolls-Royce of 4x4s is very apt. Wood and (from 1988) leather in top-specification models contribute greatly to this sense of well-being, and the Nineties' models are laden with convenience features which make them directly equivalent to luxury cars.

However, there are many aspects of the Range Rover which are not directly

	levelling strut with air suspension)	
	Anti-roll bars front and rear from 1990 (retro-fit possible on post-1985 models)	
Steering:	Power-assisted as standard	
Brakes:	Discs on all four wheels, with power assistance as standard; front discs ventilated from 1989; ABS standard on Vogue SE from 1989 and Vogue LSE, and optional on other models	
Dimensions:	Wheelbase	Standard 100in (2,540mm) Vogue LSE 108in (2,743mm)
	Length	Standard 176in (4,470mm) Vogue LSE 183in (4,648mm)
	Height	70in (1,778mm)
	Width	70in (1,778mm)
	Ground clearance	7.5in (190mm)
	Weight	Standard 3,942lb– 4,379lb (1,788kg–1,986kg), depending on model Vogue LSE 4,739lb (2,150kg)
Number of seats:	5	
Towing capacity:	8,800lb (3,990kg)	

comparable to luxury cars, and variable build quality is among them. Huge panel-gaps, ill-fitting dashboard parts and poorly matched dashboard textures and colours are among the more irritating characteristics of Range Rovers of all ages. Steering and handling are also quite different from those of conventional cars. Many people argue that the turbodiesel engines – in particular the 200 Tdi – are too noisy and unrefined to suit the Range Rover's otherwise refined nature. Further, pre-1988 models with gear-driven transfer boxes can suffer badly from transmission whine.

The rather square-rigged design now looks dated from some angles, but it has stood the test of time well and even an early Range Rover still looks distinctive among other, newer 4x4s. This agelessness has always been one of its appeals.

Performance summary

Acceleration and top speeds of the carburettor V8 and turbodiesel models are all broadly similar; among the turbodiesels, high-speed acceleration is

Insurance rating:	Tdi models	Group 12
	V8 carburettor	Group 13
	Injected V8s and 1986–1992	
	turbodiesels	Group 14
	Vogue LSE	Group 15
Fuel consumption:	3.5 carburettor	14–16mpg
	3.5 injection	17–18mpg
	3.9 petrol	18–20mpg
	4.2 petrol	17–19mpg
	2.4 turbodiesel	23–24mpg
	2.5 turbodiesel	24–25mpg
	2.5 Tdi turbodiesel	27–28mpg
Top speed:	3.5 carburettor	95mph
	3.5 injection	102mph
	3.9 petrol	110mph
	4.2 petrol	112mph
	2.4 turbodiesel	92mph
	2.5 turbodiesel	95mph
	2.5 Tdi turbodiesel	94mph
0–60mph:	3.5 carburettor	15sec
	3.5 injection	11.7sec
	3.9 petrol	11.4sec
	4.2 petrol	9.9sec
	2.4 turbodiesel	16.5sec
	2.5 turbodiesel	15.8sec
	2.5 Tdi turbodiesel	16.6sec

Already firmly established in the luxury end of the market with the Vogue and Vogue SE, the Range Rover moved even further upmarket in 1992 with the introduction of the Vogue LSE, with a 108in instead of the normal 100in wheelbase.

strongest with the Tdi engines. However, carburettor V8s with the three-speed automatic transmission are rather sluggish, and turbodiesels with the automatic transmission (available only from 1994) are also rather slow. For all-round performance, the 3.9-litre petrol V8 with automatic transmission is the best bet.

Roadholding is very secure, but Range Rovers without anti-roll bars can lean alarmingly in corners. The air-suspension models also lean more than coil-sprung types with anti-roll bars, and there are few real advantages to the air suspension except in reducing the noise transmitted from the suspension into the passenger compartment.

Off-road, all varieties of Range Rover are extremely able vehicles, capable of far more than most owners ever imagine. Low-down torque is strong with all engines, and driving aids like the viscous-coupled centre differential on post-1988 models and the Electronic Traction Control available on ABS-equipped vehicles make even the more demanding off-road work very straightforward indeed.

Reliability, weaknesses, spares
The Range Rover was already a tried-and-tested design by the time the four-door models were introduced in 1981 and few reliability problems arose in subsequent years of production. However, the engine management ECUs on injected petrol models can give trouble, the 2.4-litre and 1989–1992 2.5-litre

turbodiesels may suffer from repeated head gasket failures, and bearings sometimes fail in the pre-1994 five-speed gearboxes.

The main weaknesses lie in the suspension (where worn bushes can cause handling problems), in the complex electronics of later models (where malfunctions may be hard to trace) and in the rust which can affect the tailgates, footwells and steel inner body structure of earlier examples. Worth knowing is that damaged bonnets can be hard to repair satisfactorily and that replacements are very expensive.

Cost is always a factor in running a Range Rover, and the complexities of the later models can make professional maintenance and repair work particularly expensive. Spare parts are readily available through Land Rover dealers and through non-franchised and aftermarket outlets in the UK.

Key specification changes in the UK

1981 (Jun):	Four-door Range Rover introduced
1982 (Aug):	Three-speed automatic option introduced; special edition Range Rover Automatic In Vogue with various luxury features as standard
1983 (Jly):	Five-speed manual gearbox replaced four-speed
1983 (Aug):	Limited edition of 325 In Vogue models with choice of manual or automatic transmission and various luxury features as standard
1984 (Jun):	Injected petrol V8 introduced on Vogue models, which now became a regular production option; new instrument pack with larger instruments
1985 (Apr):	2.4-litre turbodiesel option introduced
1986 (Dec):	General facelift, including plastic grille with horizontal bars, flap over fuel filler and 60/40 split rear seat with integral head restraints; short-stick gearchange for manual models; four-speed automatic replaced three-speed; injected engine standardized on petrol models
1988 (Mar):	Vogue SE introduced, with higher specification than Vogue
1988 (Oct):	Chain-driven transfer box replaced gear-driven type
1989 (Oct):	3.9-litre engine replaced 3.5-litre; 2.5-litre turbodiesel replaced 2.4-litre in Turbo D; ABS introduced
1990 (Sep):	Limited edition of 200 two-door Range Rover CSK models, with anti-roll bars
1990 (Dec):	Anti-roll bars standardized
1992 (Oct):	Long-wheelbase Vogue LSE introduced; air suspension for top models; 200 Tdi turbodiesel engine replaced 2.5-litre
1994 (Mar):	New dashboard with airbags; new R380 five-speed manual gearbox; quieter 300 Tdi engine replaced 200 Tdi; SE trim and automatic options became available with turbodiesel engine
1994 (Oct):	Range Rover renamed Range Rover Classic on the introduction of the second-generation Range Rover

Nomenclature

Brooklands	Limited Edition of 150 with 3.9 litre V8, bodykit and Brooklands Green paintwork
CSK	Limited Edition of 200 two-door models with black paintwork and high specification level
In Vogue	Special edition Automatic (1982) and Limited Edition of 325 (1983)
Tdi	Post-1992 models with Land Rover's own 200 Tdi or 300 Tdi turbodiesel engines
Turbo D	Pre-Tdi turbodiesels with VM-built 2.4-litre (1986–1989) or 2.5-litre (1989–1992) engines
Vogue	Luxury specification
Vogue SE	Models with higher equipment levels than Vogue
Vogue LSE	Long-wheelbase models

Resale values

Depreciation is heavy on new Range Rovers, as with all luxury cars. However, resale prices have held up surprisingly well since the introduction of the second-generation models. After the initial depreciation, Range Rover values remain fairly firm until the vehicles are seven or eight years old; a sharp drop in values then reflects the likely costs of refurbishment. Early four-doors, with fairly basic equipment levels, can be bought quite cheaply.

Club information

There is a thriving club for Range Rover owners, which caters particularly for those with camping, caravanning and off-road driving interests. The Range Rover Register can be contacted via:

Les Booth
794 Lower Rainham Road
Rainham, Kent ME8 7UD

Further reading

All carburettor V8s:	*International Off-Road*, February 1994
All injected V8s:	*Off Road and 4 Wheel Drive*, December 1992
Vogue V8 5-speed:	*Off Road and 4 Wheel Drive*, December 1985
Vogue V8 Auto:	*Off Road and 4 Wheel Drive*, January 1986
Vogue SE 3.9 Auto:	*Autocar and Motor*, February 12, 1992
Vogue LSE:	*Autocar and Motor*, October 14, 1992
	Off Road and 4 Wheel Drive, November 1992
	International Off-Roader, February 1993
Turbo D (2.4):	*Off Road and 4 Wheel Drive*, June 1986
Vogue Turbo D (2.4):	*Diesel Car*, December 1988
	Autocar and Motor, August 31, 1988
Vogue Turbo D (2.5):	*Diesel Car*, May 1990
Vogue Tdi (200 Tdi):	*Diesel Car*, May 1993

RANGE ROVER
(second generation)

Background

Land Rover had a very difficult job on their hands to replace the original Range Rover, which was a widely-admired vehicle despite its age and well-known shortcomings. However, the second-generation models managed to improve on it in almost every respect, the main shortcoming being in the styling, which was very much less distinctive than the original and looked particularly undistinguished from the rear.

Part of the Range Rover's appeal had always been its remarkable off-road ability – even though only a tiny pecentage of owners ever exploited it to the full – and so the new model retained a ladder-frame chassis and beam axles. To give plenty of room inside, it had a wheelbase fractionally longer than that of the earlier Vogue LSE long-wheelbase Range Rover, and for maximum refinement it had a further developed version of the LSE's air suspension. Engines were completely reworked versions of the earlier V8s, plus a specially-adapted version of the widely acclaimed six-cylinder BMW turbodiesel.

Despite high specification levels, the entry-level price of the second-generation Range Rover was held at almost bargain levels to fight off competition from rivals like the Mitsubishi Shogun and Toyota Land Cruiser VX. The top models were nevertheless very expensive, and few of the lower-priced models were sold without several thousand pounds' worth of optional extras.

Vital statistics

Engine:	3,947cc injected petrol V8, with 190bhp at 4,750rpm and 236lb.ft at 3,000rpm or 4,554cc injected petrol V8, with 225bhp at 4,750rpm and 277lb.ft at 3,000rpm or 2,497cc turbocharged and intercooled indirect-injection six-cylinder diesel, with 134bhp at 4,400rpm and 199lb.ft at 2,300rpm
Transmission:	Four-speed automatic (petrol models), or five-speed manual (all models except 4.6 HSE)
Suspension:	Front and rear live axles, with variable rate air springs. Front axle has radius arms, Panhard rod and anti-roll bar; rear axle has trailing links and Panhard rod
Steering:	Power-assisted as standard

Brakes:	Ventilated discs at the front and solid discs at the rear; standard power assistance		
Dimensions:	Wheelbase	108.1in (2,745mm)	
	Length	185.6in (4,713mm)	
	Height	71.6in (1,817mm)	
	Width	74.4in (1,889mm)	
	Ground clearance		
	Weight	4-litre 5-speed	4,607lb (2,090kg)
		4-litre auto	4,630lb (2,100kg)
		4.6-litre	4,894lb (2,220kg)
		Turbodiesel	4,663lb (2,115kg)
Number of seats:	5		
Towing capacity:	7,700lb (3,500kg)		
Insurance rating:	Group 14 (2.5 DT)		
	Group 15 (2.5 DSE and 4.0 SE)		
	Group 16 (4.6 HSE)		
Fuel consumption:	4-litre	18mpg	
	4.6-litre	14.7mpg	
	Turbodiesel	25mpg	
Top speed:	4-litre manual	118mph	
	4-litre auto	116mph	
	4.6-litre	125mph	
	Turbodiesel	105mph	
0–60mph:	4-litre manual	9.9sec	
	4-litre auto	10.4sec	
	4.6-litre	9.3sec	
	Turbodiesel	13.3sec	

Nomenclature

DT   Base-model turbodiesels
DSE   High-line turbodiesel models
HSE   Top-of-the-range 4.6-litre models
SE   4-litre models

Character summary

The second-generation Range Rover was deliberately conceived as an alternative to conventional luxury cars, and everything about it meets the expectations of luxury-car buyers. However, it has lost none of its well-loved predecessor's underlying ruggedness or off-road ability, and has built upon existing Range Rover qualities by offering much improved road manners and

The styling of the second-generation Range Rover may be understated, but the model's status as a luxury 4x4 with rare off-road ability remains intact. This is the 4.0 V8 SE version with the smaller of the two petrol engines available in the product range.

performance. The turbodiesel models in particular offer very much greater refinement and smoother performance than the earlier turbodiesel Range Rovers.

Performance summary
The road performance of the second-generation Range Rover is exemplary; even the turbodiesel models are respectably quick. All versions are very easy to drive, with car-like controls and handling. Although these are quite large vehicles, they do not feel big in everyday use and are as well suited to town conditions as to motorway cruising.

Off the road, their performance is once again excellent, with the air suspension's automatic Extended Mode (which pushes the wheels down to make contact with the ground if traction is lost) compensating well for the handicap of the long wheelbase. However, the turbodiesel models are a little deficient on bottom-end torque.

Reliability, weaknesses, spares

These models have not been available long enough for long-term reliability problems to show up. However, some early vehicles did have teething troubles with their complex electronics, and it may be that these will prove to be a liability as the vehicles get older: certainly, they are likely to be very difficult if not impossible to maintain and repair on a DIY basis.

Spares are unlikely to prove a problem as the vehicle is supported by all Land Rover franchised dealerships. However, the cost of parts is likely to be high.

Key specification changes in the UK

1994 (Sep):   All models introduced

Resale values

The second-generation Range Rover has not yet been on sale long enough for a pattern of resale values to have become established. Early indications, however, are that resale values will remain firm for some time to come.

Further reading

All models:	*International Off-Roader*, November 1994
4.0 SE:	*Autocar and Motor*, October 5, 1994
	International Off-Roader, February 1995
4.6 HSE:	*Autocar and Motor*, September 28, 1994
	Off Road and 4 Wheel Drive, November 1994
2.5 DT:	*International Off-Roader*, February 1995
2.5 DSE:	*Diesel Car*, December 1994

Top model in the second-generation Range Rover catalogue is this impressive 4.6 HSE model, which is intended to be a viable alternative to a conventional luxury estate or saloon.

SUZUKI SJ410, SJ413, SANTANA AND SAMURAI

Background

Suzuki's SJ410 was the vehicle which really opened up the SWB four-wheel drive market in Britain during the Eighties. It offered a blend of style, fun potential, cheap purchase price and economical running costs which made it irresistible to young buyers, and it quickly became the best-selling 4x4 in Britain. Suzuki gathered the lessons it had learned from European experience of the SJ into the hugely successful Vitara, which was produced alongside the SJ after 1989, but the original range remained in demand and is still in production today, although the UK market now has only a much-reduced model range. Since early 1987, all UK-market examples of the Suzuki have been built at the Santana plant in Spain.

Suzuki was a late entrant to the world of four-wheel drives. The company's first models were built at the beginning of the Seventies, and drew on proven micro-car technology to create a miniature 4x4 for markets in South East Asia. The original LJ models were available in the UK between 1979 and 1981, but the SJ410 which reached Britain in 1982 was a version of the completely new model introduced in Japan in 1981.

The UK soon proved to be a very lucrative market for the SJ410, and in due course Suzuki GB was able to influence the actual development of the vehicle. It was the British importer, for example, which adopted the Rhino logo associated with the SJ series, and UK market demands have influenced the vehicle in a number of ways. The mid-Eighties saw the original 1-litre SJ410 supplemented by a 1.3-litre SJ413, and then the transfer of SJ410 production from Japan to Spain; subsequent SJ410s have been badged as Suzuki Santana models. SJ413 production followed suit in 1990, when the bigger-engined models were renamed the Samurai series.

The epitome of a 4x4 fun vehicle, the UK-market Suzuki SJ410s were built in Spain from 1987 onwards and carried the Santana name badge.

The Suzuki SJ series have never pretended to be heavy-duty off-roaders. They are lightweight four-wheel drive fun buggies, ideal as stylish town runabouts and inexpensive off-roaders for weekend amusement. Nevertheless, their combination of real off-road ability with all the trappings of an on-road fashion accessory blazed a trail for others to follow.

Vital statistics

Engine:	**SJ410:** 970cc carburettor petrol four-cylinder, with 45bhp at 5,500rpm and 54lb.ft at 3,000rpm
	SJ413: 1,324cc carburettor petrol four-cylinder, with 63bhp at 6,000rpm and 74lb.ft at 3,500rpm; 68bhp from April 1992
Transmission:	Four-speed manual (SJ410 to March 1987) or five-speed manual (later SJ410 and all SJ413)
	Selectable four-wheel drive
	Manually lockable freewheeling front hubs
Suspension:	Live front and rear axles; leaf springs all round; front anti-roll bar on SJ413
Steering:	Unassisted
Brakes:	Drums on all four wheels (1982–84); discs on front wheels and drums on rears (1984 on)
	Servo assistance on Santana-built SJ410 and on all SJ413

Dimensions:		
	Wheelbase	79.9in (2,030mm)
	Length	135.4in (3,440mm)
	Height	65.9in (1,675mm)
	Width	1982–1988: 60.2in (1,530mm)
		1988 on: 63in (1,600mm)
	Ground clearance	8.3in (210mm)
	Weight	Soft Top 2,028lb (920kg)
		Estate 2,072lb (940kg)

Number of seats:	4	
Towing capacity:	SJ410 five-speed 1,653lb (750kg); all other models 2,425lb (1,100kg)	
Insurance rating:	Group 6	
Fuel consumption:	SJ410 four-speed	27–37mpg
	SJ413 five-speed	27–37mpg
Top speed:	SJ410	67mph
	SJ413	74mph
0–60mph:	SJ410	27sec
	SJ413	19.4sec

The UK market has also seen limited numbers of long-wheelbase SJ models as well as several variants intended for the commercial market.

Character summary
The SJ series are unashamedly aimed at the younger buyer. They are intended to offer style and fun at low cost, and in order to do so they offer minimal size, performance and equipment levels. Optional extras can improve the latter, of course, but most SJs have a fairly basic specification.

Like most SWB four-wheel drives, the SJs offer very little luggage accommodation behind the rear seats; in fact space is at a premium throughout. Their ride comfort is poor and their engines are insufficiently powerful to make long-distance travel a comfortable experience. However, they do make for good urban runabouts, and the Soft Top versions offer excellent open-air motoring in the summer.

Hard Top models lack some of the chic appeal of the Soft Tops and are often nowadays found in a semi-commercial role rather than as everyday transport.

Performance summary
Neither the SJ410 nor the SJ413 is very quick on the road, although the bigger-engined examples can be less frustrating to drive on long journeys. The stiff springs and short wheelbase combine to give a very bumpy ride, and high noise levels help to make long-distance driving a tiring experience.

The SJ410 Estate entered the UK market in 1982, two months after the open vehicle's debut; mechanically they were identical.

At the end of the Eighties, there were scares about the SJs' handling, when consumer organizations in Britain and the USA attempted to prove that the vehicle was likely to overturn in certain conditions. Suzuki responded by widening the tracks to make the SJs more stable, but the truth is that even early SJs are unlikely to give handling problems unless severely provoked – when they are as likely to overturn as any other four-wheel drive treated with a lack of sympathy by its driver.

Off the road, the SJs give very good performance. Neither engine offers very much bottom-end torque, but in these lightweight vehicles the low gearing and large tyres are enough to compensate. The short wheelbase and short front and rear overhangs also make the SJs very agile in demanding conditions.

Reliability, weaknesses, spares

Despite their relatively flimsy construction, SJs survive very well. However, examples which have been used extensively off-road sometimes suffer damage underneath, where the mechanical elements are not very well protected. Rust also becomes a problem in older vehicles, affecting the body seams, the bumpers and the area around the door and bonnet hinges. Soft Tops do not always wear well, and their fasteners can fail.

Well-used SJs are also likely to suffer from a collection of squeaks and rattles. Sometimes, these are simply caused by items working loose and can be rectified with a screwdriver or socket spanner.

Spares are readily available from Suzuki dealers, and there is some

A relatively rare, but useful alternative to the standard-wheelbase SJ413 is this longer-wheelbase version derived from a commercial-market chassis, a number of which are to be found on the UK secondhand market.

aftermarket support for the vehicle in the provision of alternative hardtops, bull bars, wheels and other cosmetic addenda.

Key specification changes in the UK

1982 (Jun):	SJ410 introduced as Soft Top only
1982 (Aug):	SJ410 Estate introduced
1984 (Jun):	Front disc brakes added; revised (beige) interior trim and facia
1985 (May):	SJ413 introduced as Samurai VJX Estate
1986 (Apr):	High-back front seats introduced on Soft Tops, cloth upholstery for Estates
1987 (Feb):	First imports of Santana-built SJ410
1988 (Mar):	Original SJ410 Soft Top discontinued
1988 (Aug):	Five-speed gearbox replaced four-speed on SJ410; wider track and low-profile tyres; handbrake mechanism relocated from transfer box output to rear wheels
1988 (Nov):	SJ410 Santana Style Hard Top introduced
1989 (Apr):	SJ410 Santana Style Hard Top discontinued
1989 (Aug):	Limited edition SJ410 Santana Rhino; SJ413 Samurai Soft Top introduced
1990 (Apr):	SJ410 Santana Soft Top discontinued
1990 (Jly):	LWB Samurai introduced
1992 (Apr):	SJ413 engines had power increase
1992 (Jly):	SJ413 Samurai Tobago limited edition
1993 (Jly):	All models discontinued except for SJ413 Samurai Soft Top

Nomenclature

Rhino	Limited Edition of 175 white SJ410 Estates, with rhinoceros graphics
Samurai	SJ413 models
Santana	SJ410 models built by Santana in Spain
SJ410	Models with 970cc engine
SJ410 Q	Original SJ410 Soft Top (1982–1988)
SJ410 VJL	Original SJ410 Estate (1982–1988)
SJ410 VJX	Santana-built SJ410 Estate (1988–1990)
SJ413	Models with 1,324cc engine
SJ413 JX	Santana-built SJ413 Estate (1988 on)
SJ413 VJX	Original SJ413 Estate (1982–1988)
Sport	Soft Top SJ410 (1987–1990) and Hard Top SJ410 (1989–1990)
Style	Hard Top SJ410 (1988–1989)
Tobago	Limited Edition Soft Top in metallic white, with 'Rhino Surfer' side graphics and special spare-wheel cover

Resale values
For a long time, the SJ410 was the cheapest four-wheel drive vehicle available on the UK market, and although it has since been undercut by other models it

Suzuki ownership is supported by a thriving Rhino Club, which in turn has led to the introduction of a number of limited-edition vehicles, including this SJ410 Rhino Special with appropriately decorated sides.

remains a cheap vehicle. However, there is such demand for all variants that even the oldest examples have kept their value surprisingly well.

Soft Top models keep their value much better than Estate variants, and Soft Tops which come with demountable (usually aftermarket) Hard Tops are particularly desirable.

Club information
Suzuki GB set up the Rhino Club for SJ owners many years ago and this is a thriving organization which runs events of all types, including off-roading. It can be contacted through:

Suzuki GB plc
PO Box 56
Tunbridge Wells
Kent TN1 2XY
(Tel: 01892-535110)

There are also regional SJ owners' clubs.

Further reading
All models: *International Off-Roader*, April 1993
                  Off Road and 4 Wheel Drive, May 1993
SJ410 Q: *Off Road and 4 Wheel Drive*, December 1985
SJ413 VJX: *Autocar and Motor*, November 25, 1987

There is also a book entitled *Suzuki SJ: The Enthusiast's Companion*, edited by Ray Hutton and published by Motor Racing Publications.

SUZUKI VITARA

Background
Flushed with the success of the diminutive SJ models in Europe and the USA, Suzuki decided to develop a small four-wheel drive which was more consciously styled and had better road performance and handling. The result was announced in 1988 as the Vitara (or Escudo back home in Japan).

The Vitara was the first of a new breed of four-wheel drive, designed to behave like a car on the road and featuring smart styling to attract fashion-conscious buyers. Daihatsu had hit on the same idea and introduced their Sportrak at exactly the same time, but it was less adventurous than the Vitara and ultimately less successful. By the beginning of 1995, more than 800,000 Vitaras had been built, making the vehicle by far the most popular of its type worldwide. Some 34,000 examples had found buyers in Britain.

The original Vitara was developed over the years, but it has only ever been available with petrol engines: Lion Heart models using Peugeot 1.9-litre turbodiesel power are professional aftermarket conversions. The original three-door Hard Top was followed by a Soft Top (where a rear seat was an optional extra), and then LWB five-door family estates arrived in 1991. These were further enhanced when a more powerful V6-engined five-door was introduced at the end of 1994. Meanwhile, Suzuki had remorselessly tested the market for the Vitara by introducing increasingly more convenience equipment, cosmetic dress-up items and luxury options. Air conditioning and automatic transmission were unheard-of at this level of the market – but by mid-1990 they could be had on a Vitara.

Many SWB Vitaras have been extensively personalized, with accessories

The Vitara was Suzuki's way of offering a more refined alternative to the SJ models without sacrificing the fun factor. A hardtop is available for the open-top model to increase its versatility.

from Suzuki or a number of aftermarket suppliers. In that sense, the model is a direct four-wheel drive equivalent of the hot hatch saloon car, appealing to young image-conscious buyers. Suzuki have even managed to sell van versions of the SWB Vitara to commercial users – an astonishing tribute to the sheer breadth of the vehicle's market appeal.

Character summary

The Vitara is all about style and image, and its good road performance helps it to appeal to former saloon car drivers much better than most other four-

Vital statistics	
Engine:	1,590cc carburettor petrol four-cylinder, with 74bhp at 5,250rpm and 90lb.ft at 3,100rpm or 1,590cc injected petrol four-cylinder, with 80bhp at 5,400rpm and 94lb.ft at 3,000rpm (JLX SE only, from July 1991) or 1,590cc injected petrol four-cylinder, with 95bhp at 5,600rpm and 98lb.ft at 4,000rpm (LWB models only) or 1,998cc injected petrol V6, with 136bhp at 6,500rpm and 127lb.ft at 4,000rpm (LWB models only, 1995 on)
Transmission:	Five-speed manual or three-speed automatic (SE only, from April 1990); or four-speed automatic (LWB models only) Selectable four-wheel drive Manual or automatic freewheeling front hubs available as a dealer accessory; automatic type standard on LWB V6
Suspension:	Independent front suspension with struts, coil springs and anti-roll bar Live rear axle with coil springs
Steering:	Unassisted; power-assisted on JLX models
Brakes:	Discs at the front (ventilated discs on LWB V6) and drums at the rear; ABS optional on LWB V6 Estate
Dimensions:	Wheelbase SWB 86.6in (2,200mm) LWB 97.6in (2,480mm) Length SWB 142.5in (3,620mm) LWB 159in (4,038mm) LWB V6 162.7in (4,133mm) Height SWB 75.9in (1,930mm)

wheel drives. The SWB models are the direct equivalent of the hot hatch; the LWB family estates are rather more sober vehicles but offer considerably more style and image than many estate-type cars and four-wheel drives of similar cost. The latest LWB V6 is exceptional in this field.

However, there is world of difference between the fun-appeal of a Vitara Soft Top with only two seats and the stylish practicality of a LWB five-door family estate. Also, many Vitara drivers tend to ignore the vehicle's off-road capability, being too proud of the gleaming paintwork and array of custom extras ever to dream of getting them muddy.

Width		LWB 66.7in (1,695mm)
		Four-cyl models 64in (1,625mm)
		V6 LWB models 66.3in (1,685mm)
Ground clearance		7.9in (200mm)
Weight		SWB Soft Top 2,115lb (959kg)
		SWB Estate 2,180lb (988kg)
		SWB JLX SE 2,345lb (1,063kg)
		LWB 3,637lb (1,650kg)
		LWB V6 Manual 2,888lb (1,310kg)
		LWB V6 Auto 2,932lb (1,330kg)
Number of seats:	SWB	5
	LWB	5
Towing capacity:	SWB	3,195lb (1,450kg)
	LWB	3,300lb (1,500kg)
	LWB V6	Not quoted by Suzuki GB
Insurance rating:	Group 8	
Fuel consumption:	SWB	26–32mpg
	LWB	25–31mpg
Top speed:	SWB	95mph
	LWB	98mph
	LWB V6	99mph (manual) 93mph (auto)
0–60mph:	SWB	17.2sec
	SWB SE	16sec
	LWB	14.1sec
	LWB V6	12.5sec (manual) } figures for 14sec (auto) } 0–62mph

Performance summary

Despite the sporting appeal of its high-revving 16-valve petrol engine, the four-cylinder Vitara is not a fast road machine, except by comparison with other four-wheel drives. It is quick enough, though, and the LWB V6 is quicker again. Both types will happily cruise at well above the UK motorway limit without undue noise.

Ride comfort is excellent, although many owners fit wide, low-profile tyres which can cause the ride quality to become harsh. Such tyres can also increase the vehicles' tendency to aquaplane in the wet, although normally they give no cause for concern in this respect. Towing is not one of the SWB Vitara's stronger suits.

The low ground clearance of the Vitara improves its handling on the road at the expense of some off-road ability. Nevertheless, it is really quite able in the rough, with the short wheelbase, short overhangs and good axle articulation contributing to a much better performance than its appearance suggests. However, poor engine braking does limit the Vitara's ability to descend steep hills under safe control when off-road.

Reliability, weaknesses, spares

The Vitara is a well-built machine in the best Japanese tradition. The four-cylinder models have no known faults; the V6s are too new to be properly evaluated, although they are most unlikely to prove less reliable or well-made than the older types.

In 1991 the Vitara JLX SE's 1.6-litre engine graduated from carburettor to fuel injection, bringing a useful 8 per cent improvement in maximum power.

The JLX SE five-door estate, based on a 11in longer wheelbase, considerably expanded the Vitara's customer base following its introduction in 1991.

However, it is advisable to check modified vehicles very thoroughly before buying. Wide wheels and tyres, for example, can in some cases lead to accelerated wear on suspension components. Similarly, some GRP body panels may develop cracks or crazing after a time.

Spares are available through the Suzuki dealer network, which also markets a wide range of accessories. There is a substantial aftermarket for the Vitara.

Key specification changes in the UK

1988 (Oct):   Estate introduced to UK
1989 (Jly):   Soft Top added to range
1989 (Dec):   JLX SE Estate added to range
1990 (Apr):   Automatic transmission option introduced
1991 (Jun):   Injected engine with catalytic converter replaced carburettor type; revised trim for SE models
1991 (Sep):   LWB models added to range
1993 (May):   Vitara Sport entry-level model introduced
1993 (Jly):   Electric sunroof option for LWB models
1993 (Oct):   Entry-level JX LWB model introduced
1994 (Dec):   V6 LWB added to range
1995 (Feb):   Sport 2 introduced

Nomenclature

JLX   Standard models
JLX SE   High-line models

139

JX	Entry-level LWB models
Mustique	July 1992 limited edition, based on SWB Soft Top or Estate, with white paint and Rhino; Desert Island graphics on sides and bonnet
Rossini	March 1994 limited edition, based on Sport, with metallic magenta paint, white hood and trim
SE Executive	December 1990 limited edition SE Estate with air conditioning, leather upholstery and wood trim
Sport	Entry-level Soft Top models
Verdi	January 1994 limited edition Sport Soft Top, with rear seat, special upholstery and metallic green paint
X-EC	July 1993 limited edition, based on LWB JLX SE, with black paint, flared wheelarches, alloy wheels and limited-slip differential

Resale values

Vitaras are in such demand that there is a seller's market. As a result, high prices are asked and paid, and resale values are firm. Examples with extra equipment – including aftermarket cosmetic add-ons – may command a hefty price premium over showroom-standard vehicles.

The prices of Soft Top models tend to be higher in the summer, while the prices of SWB Estates tend to be higher in the winter. LWB models are not subject to these seasonal fluctuations.

Club information

The Suzuki Rhino Club runs events of all types, including off-roading. It can be contacted through:

Suzuki GB plc
PO Box 56
Tunbridge Wells
Kent TN1 2XY
(Tel: 01892-535110)

Further reading

All models:	*International Off-Roader*, November 1993
SWB JLX:	*Autocar and Motor*, March 29, 1989
	Off Road and 4 Wheel Drive, December 1994
Soft Top JLX SE:	*International Off-Roader*, November 1992
Soft Top Sport:	*Off Road and 4 Wheel Drive*, August 1993
LWB JLX SE:	*Off Road and 4 Wheel Drive*, October 1991
	International Off-Roader, December 1991
LWB X-EC:	*Off Road and 4 Wheel Drive*, February 1994

Also available is the book entitled *Suzuki Vitara: The Enthusiast's Companion* by Nigel Fryatt, published by Motor Racing Publications.

TOYOTA 4-RUNNER

Background

Although the Toyota 4-Runner was introduced to the UK as a new vehicle in 1993, it was introduced to its Japanese home market in 1989 under the name of the Hi-Lux Surf. A few examples were brought into the UK as personal imports in the early Nineties, and these have a slightly different specification from the 'genuine' UK-market vehicles; some also have different engines.

The concept behind the 4-Runner is very simple. The vehicle is actually based on a modified four-wheel drive Hi-Lux pick-up chassis (hence the Japanese market name), and it shares much of the Hi-Lux's styling. The chassis modifications are mainly to the suspension, which substitutes a coil-sprung rear end for the pick-up's harsh leaf springs – and, of course, the 4-Runner has much more powerful and refined engines.

Sales of this distinctive long-wheelbase family 4x4 have been disappointingly slow in the UK, and it deserves very much better despite certain undeniable drawbacks.

Character summary

One of the 4-Runner's strengths is its styling, which combines the overall appearance of a car-derived estate with the stance of a four-wheel drive and a rugged frontal design derived from that of the big Land Cruiser VX. Refinement is another strength, and there is plenty of load space in the rear of the body. Toyota GB have so far failed to promote the vehicle effectively as the stylish family estate which it undoubtedly is.

The 4-Runner's main drawbacks are a lack of passenger headroom, brought about by its low build, and a truck-like driving position which comes from the Hi-Lux range on which it is based.

Performance summary

Among other four-wheel drive estates, the 4-Runner stands out as an exceptionally good road vehicle. The V6 petrol engine is extremely flexible and smooth, while the turbodiesel gives both good performance and exemplary refinement. The ride quality is as good as that in a conventional saloon-derived estate, and handling is stable with little body roll. The 4-Runner also makes a stable and powerful tow vehicle.

Off the road, the 4-Runner feels strong and solid. Its long wheelbase, side steps and long rear overhang are handicaps, but both engines have plenty of controllable low-down torque. The coil spring suspension also gives a good ride over rough terrain.

Reliability, weaknesses, spares

Toyota have an excellent reputation for reliability and there is no reason to suppose that the 4-Runner will prove an exception. Certainly, build quality is up to the usual very high standard, and Toyota should have ironed out any teething troubles with the model long ago. However, it is too early to make a reliable evaluation of UK examples, which have been available for only just over a year at the time of writing.

Spares are available through Toyota dealerships. There are no aftermarket suppliers for the 4-Runner in the UK.

Vital statistics

Engine: 2,959cc injected petrol V6, with 141bhp at 4,600rpm and 171lb.ft at 3,400rpm
or 2,982cc direct-injection turbodiesel four-cylinder, with 123bhp at 3,600rpm and 217lb.ft at 2,000rpm

Transmission: Five-speed manual
Selectable four-wheel drive
Automatic Disconnecting Differential in front axle
Limited-slip differential in rear axle

Suspension: Independent front suspension with twin wishbones, torsion bar springs and anti-roll bar; four-link independent rear suspension with coil springs and anti-roll bar

Steering: Power-assisted as standard

Brakes: Ventilated discs at the front; drums at the rear; power-assisted

Dimensions:
Wheelbase	103.3in (2,625mm)
Length	176.7in (4,490mm)
Height	69in (1,755mm)
Width	70.5in (1,790mm)
Ground clearance	8.7in (220mm)
Weight	Petrol models 4,056lb (1,840kg) Turbodiesel models 4,189lb (1,900kg)

Number of seats: 4/5
Towing capacity: 4,850lb (2,200kg)
Insurance rating: Group 12

Fuel consumption:
Petrol models	13–23mpg
Turbodiesel models	20–30mpg

Top speed:
Petrol models	103mph
Turbodiesel models	93mph

0–60mph:
Petrol models	15.1sec
Turbodiesel models	16.4sec

Toyota' 4-Runner, available with 3-litre V6 petrol or four-cylinder turbodiesel engine, has estate-car styling on a modified pick-up chassis.

Key specification changes in the UK
1993 (Oct): Range introduced to UK

Resale values
Too few examples of the 4-Runner have appeared on the secondhand market for it to be possible to make a reliable assessment of the model's resale value. However, early indications are that values are likely to be firm, and that depreciation will be rather lower than average for this type of vehicle.

Other information
There are two clubs for Toyota owners in the UK. The one run by the importers is the Toyota Owners' Club, which can be contacted through:

Toyota (GB) Ltd
The Quadrangle
Station Road
Redhill
Surrey RH1 1PX
(Tel: 017377-68585)

There is also the Toyota Enthusiasts' Club, whose contact is:

Billy Wells
28 Park Road
Feltham
Middlesex TW13 6PW

Further reading
All models: *Off Road and 4 Wheel Drive*, December 1993
V6 petrol: *International Off-Roader*, September 1994

With a good ride from its coil-spring suspension and ample torque available from either engine the 4-Runner offers very good towing performance.

TOYOTA LAND CRUISER II

Background

Although the Toyota Land Cruiser II reached the UK in 1988, it had been on sale in other markets since the mid-Eighties. The Land Cruiser II designation is unique to the UK; in other markets, the model is simply the short-wheelbase variant of the vast J7 series, of which a few long-wheelbase examples reached Britain as personal imports in the Nineties.

The Land Cruiser II's basic specification is conventional and typically Japanese, with a rigid ladder-frame chassis, a steel-panelled body, selectable four-wheel drive and manually lockable front hubs. All-round coil spring suspension made the vehicle stand out from its rivals in Britain in the late Eighties, although it is less unusual now.

From the beginning, Toyota (GB) have aimed the Land Cruiser II at a very clearly-defined niche market, essentially one where buyers are prepared to pay relatively high prices for a short-wheelbase four-wheel drive. This means that the standard turbodiesel engine (which was uprated in 1993) is complemented by a high level of standard equipment, including power-assisted steering, electric windows, an electric sunroof and chromed side steps.

With a specification like that, the vehicle has a limited but definite appeal. Fewer than 3,000 examples had found buyers in the UK by the end of 1994. Despite Toyota's hints to the contrary, it is unlikely that more vehicles with this specification would find buyers in the UK even if the company did not operate (like other Japanese manufacturers) under a quota agreement which limits the number of vehicles it is allowed to import in any one year.

With the Land Cruiser II Toyota has offered the 4x4 market a turbodiesel-engined short-wheelbase vehicle with a higher than usual specification.

Character summary

Despite the high levels of standard equipment, everything about the Land Cruiser II reminds driver and passengers that this is a vehicle built for rough-terrain work in Africa which has been adapted to Western city life. Its solid feel is immensely reassuring, but in truth the vehicle's appeal in the UK has more to do with its rugged image.

The interior is surprisingly drab, with an untidily laid out dashboard and a gimmicky collection of instruments (including an altimeter!) in a central pod.

Vital statistics

Engine:	2,446cc turbodiesel four-cylinder, with 84bhp at 4,000rpm and 138lb.ft at 2,400rpm (1988–1990), or 88bhp at 3,500rpm and 158lb.ft at 2,400rpm (1990–1993) or 2,982cc direct-injection turbodiesel four-cylinder, with 123bhp at 3,600rpm and 217lb.ft at 2,000rpm
Transmission:	Five-speed manual Selectable four-wheel drive Manually lockable freewheeling front hubs Limited-slip differentials front and rear
Suspension:	Live front axle with coil springs and anti-roll bar Live rear axle with coil springs and trailing links
Steering:	Power assisted as standard
Brakes:	Discs at the front and drums at the rear; Power assistance standard

Dimensions:		
	Wheelbase	90.9in (2,310mm)
	Length	161in (4,090mm)
	Height	75.9in (1,930mm)
	Width	71in (1,803mm)
	Ground clearance	8.7in (220mm)
	Weight	2.4-litre: 3,990lb (1,810kg) 3-litre: 4,140lb (1,878kg)

Number of seats:	4/5	
Towing capacity:	4,410lb (2,000kg)	
Insurance rating:	Group 12	
Fuel consumption:	2.4-litre:	18–28mpg
	3-litre:	18–28mpg
Top speed:	2.4-litre	85mph
	3-litre	93mph
0–60mph:	2.4-litre	23.9sec
	3-litre:	16.4sec

The Land Cruiser II has been available with a choice of 2.4-litre and 3-litre four-cylinder turbodiesel engines and a five-speed manual gearbox.

The front seats of the Land Cruiser II are comfortable enough for long journeys, but the rear seat is narrow, able to take three abreast only in some discomfort. The load space behind it is as limited as in many smaller SWB four-wheel drives.

Performance summary

The best of the three engines fitted to the Land Cruiser II is the latest 3-litre turbodiesel, which offers much better acceleration and higher cruising speeds than the earlier 2.4-litre types. The original 2.4-litre is the weakest of all; the later version available between 1990 and 1993 offers worthwhile improvements in driveability. The gearchange on all versions is slick and positive.

Despite a certain amount of pitching, the ride quality is generally good. However, there is plenty of body roll in corners, and the steering is too light for some tastes – a combination which means that the Land Cruiser II sometimes needs acclimatization before it can be driven with confidence.

Off-road, the Land Cruiser II performs very well indeed, aided in extreme conditions by its front and rear axle differential locks. However, the standard tyres are rather too wide to give the best traction in some conditions.

Reliability, weaknesses, spares

Everything about the Land Cruiser II is durable and reliable, and the build quality is up to Toyota's familiar high standard. Despite the steel body, rust has not been a problem on UK-market examples. Spares back-up from Toyota dealerships is first-class and parts are not particularly expensive.

There is very little aftermarket support for these vehicles, mainly because of the small numbers in the UK.

Key specification changes in the UK

1988 (May): First imports of Land Cruiser II
1990 (May): More rounded styling introduced; honeycomb grille replaced by grille with horizontal bars; power and torque of engine increased
1993 (Aug): 3-litre engine replaced 2.4-litre type

Resale values

Depreciation on these Land Cruisers seems to be about average for this type of vehicle, because their above-average durability is offset by relatively small numbers of interested buyers. The earliest examples now sell for about 35 per cent of the price of a showroom-fresh vehicle, and their prices will continue to fall as more examples of the very much better 3-litre models come onto the secondhand market.

Other information

Owners of a Land Cruiser II are eligible to join three UK clubs. Specifically for the vehicle is the Land Cruiser 4x4 Club, which can be contacted through Joe Boatwright on 01793-497366. The Toyota Owners' Club is run by the importers, Toyota (GB) Ltd, and can be contacted at:

The Quadrangle
Station Road
Redhill
Surrey RH1 1PX
(Tel: 017377-68585)

The Toyota Enthusiasts' Club is an independent organization, whose contact is:

Billy Wells
28 Park Road
Feltham
Middlesex TW13 6PW

Further reading

2.4-litre (84bhp): *Off Road and 4 Wheel Drive*, June 1988
Diesel Car, December 1988
2.4-litre (88bhp): *Diesel Car*, November 1991
International Off-Roader, March 1992
2.4-litre (both types): *Off Road and 4 Wheel Drive*, October 1993
International Off-Roader, March 1994
3-litre: *Off Road and 4 Wheel Drive*, March 1994
International Off-Roader, June 1994

TOYOTA LAND CRUISER LWB
(first generation)

Background

Toyota made no real impact on the British four-wheel drive market until the early Eighties, even though the Land Cruiser had been around in various forms since 1954 and went on to become the world's best-selling light 4x4. Introduced in Japan during 1980, the 60-series long-wheelbase models were brought to Britain early in 1982 (after a summer 1981 preview). So, although they represent the first-generation Land Cruiser to British buyers, they are very far from being the first Land Cruisers.

Although the Land Cruiser had something in common with contemporaries like the Mitsubishi Shogun, it was a very much more rugged and utilitarian vehicle and was not fine-tuned to suit the family estate 4x4 market until later in the decade. The Land Cruiser's market was primarily that of the Land Rover Station Wagon utilities; originally developed as a dirt-road vehicle for underdeveloped countries, it was best suited in Britain to business users rather than family buyers.

The first-generation Land Cruiser's specification was unexceptional, with a ladder-frame chassis and beam axles with leaf springs all round. For the UK, it came only as a four-door estate with a big six-cylinder diesel engine, although other markets were offered different engines. The UK specification was completed by a number of items from the Toyota options list: reclining front seats with head restraints and cloth upholstery, an adjustable steering column, a heated rear window with wash/wipe, and a radio.

The first specification change came in 1983, when the original four-speed manual gearbox was replaced by a five-speed. A four-speed overdrive automatic was briefly available during 1985, but failed to arouse much interest and was quickly withdrawn. A more comprehensive package of specification changes in 1987 produced the GX models, which were rather better suited than earlier vehicles to the demands of the family market.

Vital statistics

Engine:	3,980cc indirect-injection diesel six-cylinder, with 99bhp at 3,500rpm and 176lb.ft at 2,300rpm (1982–1987), or 101bhp at 3,500rpm and 178lb.ft at 2,300rpm (1987–1990)
Transmission:	Four-speed manual (to March 1983) or five-speed manual (from April 1983)

	Optional four-speed automatic (1985 only)	
	Selectable four-wheel drive	
	Manually lockable freewheeling front hubs	
Suspension:	Live front and rear axles with semi-elliptic leaf springs	
Steering:	Power-assisted as standard	
Brakes:	Discs on the front wheels and drums at the rear	
Dimensions:	Wheelbase	108in (2,743mm)
	Length	184in (4,674mm)
	Height	71in (1,803mm)
	Width	71in (1,803mm)
	Ground clearance	7.3in (185mm)
	Weight	4,453lb (2,020kg)
Number of seats:	5	
Towing capacity:	7,715lb (3,500kg)	
Insurance rating:	Group 12	
Fuel consumption:	15–25mpg	
Top speed:	89mph	
0–60mph:	23.6sec	

The first long-wheelbase Land Cruisers to enter the UK market were capacious but essentially utilitarian vehicles for the business user.

Character summary

The first-generation Land Cruiser is a big vehicle in all respects, offering a vast carrying capacity. However, it also feels big, and some drivers find that its size is somewhat intimidating. Its styling, always rather truck-like, has not dated very well.

The low-down pulling power of the big diesel engine, and the vehicle's great weight and stability give these Land Cruisers excellent towing abilities. However, not even the added creature comforts of the post-1987 GX models can disguise the fact that the first-generation Land Cruiser was designed for parts of the world where roads are few and ruggedness is the primary requirement in a vehicle. That ruggedness undeniably provides a great deal of character, although it is unlikely to suit those whose requirement is for a reasonably sophisticated four-wheel-drive family estate.

Performance summary

The big diesel engine provides relaxed performance, with excellent flexibility from its wide torque band. It is powerful enough to keep a Land Cruiser cruising comfortably for long periods at speeds in excess of the UK motorway limit, but it offers only leisurely acceleration from rest. The slow gearchange is no help here.

Steering is light at parking speeds, but can feel vague when the vehicle is on the move. Soft springing allows quite a lot of body roll on corners, and the brakes are only adequately powerful for such a heavy vehicle and will not reassure nervous drivers. The Land Cruiser's braking system was designed with a load-sensing valve in the rear hydraulic line to cope with a heavily-laden vehicle, and as a result these vehicles tend to stop rather more positively when fully laden.

Off-road, bottom-end torque from the big diesel engine makes light work of steep inclines, but the vehicle's overall size and its long wheelbase do work against it in many situations. The long rear overhang, with the spare wheel below it, can also make life off-road difficult. Axle articulation is good for a leaf-sprung vehicle, but the soft springs can cause a bouncy, wallowy ride on rough terrain.

Reliability, weaknesses, spares

Build quality and durability are first-rate, and the engine is a particularly long-lived unit if it is regularly serviced. However, the all-steel body does rust as it gets older – in the lower tailgate, around the tailgate window, in the body sills, around the wheelarches, in the roof gutters and just above the hinges in the front doors. Trim is hard-wearing, but many early Land Cruisers have been used very hard and some will have scruffy interiors as a result.

Spares are available through Toyota dealers, but they are not cheap.

Key specification changes in the UK

1981 (Jly):   Introduced to UK
1983 (Apr):   Five-speed gearbox replaced four-speed

1985 (Mar):	Automatic option introduced
1985 (Dec):	Automatic option discontinued
1987 (Nov):	Specification changes produced GX model: four rectangular headlamps replaced two round ones, larger front bumper, chrome wheels, curved facia, electric windows, central locking, radio/cassette replaced radio, intermittent rear wash/wipe
1990 (May):	Range replaced by Land Cruiser VX

Nomenclature

GX   Upgraded post-1987 models

Resale values

Depreciation on these Land Cruisers is only average, although the earliest examples are now available quite cheaply. Even the newest models are not expensive purchases. One reason why values have not dropped further is undoubtedly that the newer Land Cruiser VX is aimed at a very different clientele; secondhand examples are therefore not affecting the prices of the older models. In the longer term, condition and fitness for service will probably come to affect prices more than the vehicle's age, just as they do on a Land Rover.

Other information

There are three clubs for Land Cruiser owners in the UK. Specifically for the vehicle is the Land Cruiser 4x4 Club, which can be contacted through Joe Boatwright on 01793-497366. The importers run the Toyota Owners' Club, which can be contacted through Toyota (GB) Ltd, at:

The Quadrangle
Station Road
Redhill
Surrey RH1 1PX
(Tel: 017377-68585)

There is also the Toyota Enthusiasts' Club, whose contact is:

Billy Wells
28 Park Road
Feltham
Middlesex TW13 6PW

Further reading

All models:	*Off Road and 4 Wheel Drive*, November 1992
	International Off-Roader, October 1993
	Off Road and 4 Wheel Drive, December 1993
Early models:	*Motor*, November 14, 1981
	Off Road and 4 Wheel Drive, May 1985

TOYOTA LAND CRUISER VX

Background

The Land Cruiser VX has a very different character from any other model which has worn Land Cruiser badges, and yet it retains all the legendary ruggedness and rough-terrain abilities of its predecessors. Where it differs from them is in its complexity and sophistication, and by developing it in those two areas Toyota deliberately promoted the top-model Land Cruisers into the luxury off-roader market dominated worldwide by the Range Rover.

The Land Cruiser VX was announced in Japan in 1989 as an addition to the Land Cruiser range (more basic LWB models are still in production for many markets), and was announced in the UK during 1990. Toyota GB have always promoted it as a niche-market vehicle, offering only a big turbodiesel engine combined with a very high level of standard equipment which makes the Land Cruiser an alternative not only to turbodiesel but also to petrol-engined versions of the Range Rover. In other markets, the vehicle is available with a 215bhp six-cylinder petrol engine of 4,477cc.

The basis of the Land Cruiser VX is a traditional ladder-frame chassis with beam axles; but coil spring suspension is used in place of the leaf springs on earlier Land Cruisers. Instead of the older models' elderly pushrod-operated, naturally-aspirated indirect-injection diesel engine, there is a turbocharged diesel with a belt-driven overhead camshaft and a more efficient direct injection design. Permanent four-wheel drive has also replaced the older models' selectable system.

The Land Cruiser VX is Toyota's flagship for the luxury end of the 4x4 market; it is powered by a 4.2-litre six-cylinder turbodiesel engine.

Character summary

The Land Cruiser's appeal lies in its image and very real abilities. That image is promoted by the styling, which makes the vehicle appear large and aggressive – and there is no doubting that it is large. Dimensionally, it is the largest four-wheel drive estate available in the UK at the time of writing, which can make it something of a liability when looking for parking spaces in busy towns. Nevertheless, its size and weight, plus the enormous pulling power of the turbodiesel engine, make it a superb tow vehicle, and – unlike earlier Land Cruisers – it does not feel like a big vehicle in most circumstances.

The Land Cruiser is remarkably refined in every respect, and its high levels

Vital statistics

Engine:	4,164cc direct-injection turbodiesel six-cylinder, with 165bhp at 3,600rpm and 266lb.ft at 1,800rpm (1990–1992) or 4,164cc direct-injection turbodiesel six-cylinder, with 158bhp at 3,600rpm and 266lb.ft at 1,800rpm (1992 on)
Transmission:	Five-speed manual or four-speed automatic Permanent four-wheel drive Differential locks front, centre and rear
Suspension:	Live front and rear axles, with coil springs; front axle with leading arms and Panhard rod, rear axle with trailing links and anti-roll bar
Steering:	Power-assisted as standard
Brakes:	Discs all round (enlarged in 1992); ABS standard from 1992

Dimensions:

Wheelbase	112.2in (2,850mm)	
Length	188.3in (4,780mm)	
Height	74.5in (1,890mm)	
Width	74.9in (1,900mm)	
Ground clearance 8.3in (210mm)		
Weight	Manual	5,302lb (2,405kg)
	Auto	5,379lb (2,440kg)

Number of seats:	7
Towing capacity:	7,715lb (3,500kg)
Insurance rating:	Group 13
Fuel consumption:	20.6mpg
Top speed:	101mph
0–60mph:	Manual 15.8sec
	Auto 16.6sec

Visible changes to the Land Cruiser VX towards the end of 1992 included different alloy wheels and lower-profile tyres.

of standard equipment help it to keep company with the very best luxury four-wheel drives. It is a spacious load-carrier and will accommodate up to seven passengers in three rows of forward-facing seats. However, legroom in the centre row is only adequate and the rear seats are best reserved for children.

Performance summary

The big turbodiesel engine is smooth and responsive, although never quite as refined as the best petrol power units, and it offers as much road performance as most drivers could want. The automatic transmission is preferable to the manual, which has a rather slow change action.

Steering is light but positive, and the Land Cruiser's great weight and rigid construction help the coil springs to give a smooth ride on most surfaces. Handling is secure, within the limitations imposed by the vehicle's size, and the brakes – uprated in 1992 when ABS was standardized – are first-class.

Off-road, size is again the vehicle's biggest handicap, and the long wheelbase and long overhangs can cause difficulties. The vehicle's weight can also be a problem on very soft ground. However, the long-travel suspension gives very good axle articulation and excellent ride comfort in the rough, and the three differential locks enable traction to be maintained in most conditions. The engine's enormous bottom-end torque is another strong point, but a rather tall first gear in automatic models reduces engine braking and control for steep descents.

Reliability, weaknesses, spares

These Land Cruisers have proved every bit as reliable as the older models and there is no reason to suppose that they will be any less durable over high mileages despite their more complicated design. No recurrent weaknesses have shown up. Spares are available from the large Toyota dealership network, but there is no aftermarket in the UK.

Key specification changes in the UK

1990 (May): Range introduced to UK
1991 (Feb): Automatic telescopic radio aerial standardized
1992 (Nov): Engine changes resulted in small power loss; 16-inch alloy wheels with low-profile tyres replaced 15-inch type; larger brake discs; ABS standardized; side impact beams added; automatic models now had leather upholstery, air conditioning and power front seat adjustment as standard

Resale values

Resale values of the Land Cruiser VX are strong, and there is a healthy market demand for the vehicle.

Other information

There are three clubs for Land Cruiser owners in the UK, although most enthusiast owners tend to have the older models. The Land Cruiser 4x4 Club can be contacted through Joe Boatwright on 01793-497366. The importers run the Toyota Owners' Club, which can be contacted through:

Toyota (GB) Ltd
The Quadrangle
Station Road
Redhill
Surrey RH1 1PX (Tel: 017377-68585)

There is also the Toyota Enthusiasts' Club, whose contact is:

Billy Wells
28 Park Road
Feltham
Middlesex TW13 6PW

Further reading

Manual: *Diesel Car*, November 1990
              Autocar and Motor, February 6, 1991
              International Off-Roader, December 1992
              Off Road and 4 Wheel Drive, November 1994
Automatic: *Off Road and 4 Wheel Drive*, March 1993
              Diesel Car, June 1993

TOYOTA RAV-4

Background

With the RAV-4, Toyota confronted one of the great hypocrisies of the four-wheel drive market. Recognizing that only a small proportion of owners actually use their vehicles in demanding off-road conditions, the company designed this new model with all the style and chic of a leisure-market 4x4, but left out the transfer box which gives a second set of low-ratio gears. In spite of this, the RAV-4 still retained quite enough off-road ability to meet the demands of the occasional recreational off-road driver.

The vehicle's name embodies the ideas behind it, standing for Recreational Active Vehicle, Four-Wheel Drive. It was first shown as a concept car at the 1989 Tokyo Motor Show, then again in heavily altered form at the 1993 show. The response persuaded Toyota to put the vehicle into production, and it was announced for sale at the Geneva Motor Show in March 1994. Initially available only as a SWB three-door model, the RAV-4 was also shown in LWB five-door guise at the 1995 Geneva Motor Show. This version has not gone on sale in the UK at the time of writing.

The initials stand for Recreational Active Vehicle and this 2-litre petrol-engined 4x4 is intended for on-road and not-too-exacting off-road duties, hence the lack of a transfer box in the transmission and the use of monocoque construction instead of the usual separate chassis.

The RAV-4's mission is to broaden the market for four-wheel drive vehicles by adding more sporting appeal and removing unwanted complications. The sporting appeal comes through fashionable styling, the 2-litre petrol engine and all-independent car-type suspension; the unwanted complications (for many buyers) are the low-ratio gears and the separate chassis traditional in the off-roader market: the RAV-4 has a monocoque bodyshell. In other respects, the RAV-4 is following in the footsteps of the hugely successful Suzuki Vitara – but it has taken the ideas behind that vehicle a stage further.

Character summary
The RAV-4 is a remarkable vehicle, adding the fashionable visual appeal of a hot hatch saloon car to the big-wheeled chunky aggressiveness of a traditional off-roader. In this, it combines the functions of stylish city runabout with those

---

Vital statistics

Engine:	1,998cc injected 16-valve four-cylinder petrol, with 129bhp at 5,000rpm and 129lb.ft at 4,600rpm
Transmission:	Five-speed manual or four-speed automatic No low-range transfer box Permanent four-wheel drive Lockable, viscous-coupled centre differential
Suspension:	Independent front suspension, with McPherson struts, coil springs and anti-roll bar; independent rear suspension with twin wishbones and coil springs
Steering:	Power-assisted as standard
Brakes:	Ventilated front discs and rear drums, with power assistance
Dimensions:	Wheelbase 86.6in (2,200mm) Length 145.8in (3,705mm) Height 65in (1,650mm) Width 67in (1,702mm) Ground clearance 8.1in (205mm) Weight 3,300lb (1,497kg)
Number of seats:	4
Towing capacity:	3,307lb (1,500kg)
Insurance rating:	Group 9
Fuel consumption:	28.2mpg
Top speed:	Manual 108mph Automatic 106mph
0–60mph:	Manual 10.7sec Automatic 11.5sec

Station Wagons on both wheelbases are spacious, and the LWB models make very stable tow vehicles.

Performance summary

For long-distance work, the turbodiesel models are a better choice than the naturally-aspirated models, which tend to struggle on motorway gradients. Steering and handling are both ponderous, but the ride quality is surprisingly good for a leaf-sprung vehicle. The brakes are powerful, although the brake pedal is awkwardly placed.

Off-road, the naturally-aspirated models perform better, as the turbodiesels have taller overall gearing and their off-boost performance is relatively poor. The standard-wheelbase model has usefully short front and rear overhangs, but the LWB vehicle is too big to be very agile and its long wheelbase can cause difficulties. Both types have good under-axle clearance.

Reliability, weaknesses, spares

The Alter II has a history of minor problems, although the Peugeot-built diesel and turbodiesel engines seem to be both reliable and durable. Variable build quality is one cause of the vehicle's problems, but there are particular weaknesses in the front axle ball swivels, the door hinges, the pivot shaft for the High/Low and four-wheel drive selector levers, the speedometer cable and even the brake pads and shoes. Noise from the front springs is also common (caused by lateral movement of the springs in their mountings), but seems not to be a cause for concern.

Spares have been available through the relatively small UMM dealer network, but the parts numbering system can cause confusion and there have often been delays when non-stock parts have had to be ordered from Portugal. Now that imports have ceased, it is unclear whether parts will become difficult to obtain in the UK. There is no aftermarket support for the Alter II, although this position may well change if the dealer network is disbanded.

Key specification changes in the UK

1989 (Sep): First UK imports of Alter II; no passenger-carrying variants available
1990 (Jan): First UK imports of standard-wheelbase Turbo Diesel Station Wagon
1991 (Oct): LWB Station Wagon joined the range
1994 (Dec): Alter II no longer available in UK

Resale values

The question mark over the marque's future in the UK has weakened resale values to some extent. Demand for the Station Wagon models is also relatively weak. Nevertheless, it is still not possible to find an Alter II Station Wagon of any kind for sale cheaply: the vehicles are appreciated by those buyers who are attracted to them.

Other information
The UMM Owners' Club can be contacted through:

Glen Jones
8 Elworth Road
Elworth
Sandbach
Cheshire CW11 9HQ
(Tel: 01270-768522)

Further reading
All models: *International Off-Roader*, June 1994
SWB turbodiesel
Station Wagon: *International Off-Roader*, June 1993

The UMM Alter II long-wheelbase station wagon was available in the UK for just over three years from the autumn of 1991. Lacking in frills they may be, but the popularity of these vehicles amongst serious off-road enthusiasts is such that they sustain an active owner's club.

VAUXHALL FRONTERA

Background

The Vauxhall Frontera has never been quite what it seems. Despite its British badging (or German Opel badging in continental Europe), and even though it is assembled in Britain, it is actually Japanese in origin.

In fact, the Frontera is based on two separate models designed by Isuzu; Vauxhall's owners, the American giant General Motors, have a large share in the Japanese company and arranged the badge-engineering deal as a quick way of getting into the booming European four-wheel drive market in the early Nineties. The Frontera's arrival was quickly followed by the introduction of the Vauxhall Monterey, which again wears Opel badges on the European continent and is again actually a Japanese Isuzu design.

The short-wheelbase Frontera Sport started life as an Isuzu MU (Mysterious Utility), which is known in some markets as an Isuzu Amigo and was announced in January 1989. The long-wheelbase Frontera Estate is an MU derivative which started life as the Isuzu Rodeo and was first seen in January 1991. The Frontera editions of both models were announced in March 1991.

For their first four years as Vauxhall/Opel models, the Fronteras had European engines which generally lacked sparkle. However, revisions in 1995 brought vastly better power units (including an Isuzu turbodiesel) as well as a whole series of revisions which answered criticisms of the earlier models.

Based on an Isuzu design, the Vauxhall Frontera has achieved a considerable presence in the UK 4x4 market, this long-wheelbase model with a choice of petrol and turbodiesel engines being aimed firmly at the family market.

The overall layout of the Fronteras is typically Japanese, with steel bodies bolted to a ladder-frame chassis which has independent front suspension by torsion bars and wishbones. The original leaf-sprung live rear axle was replaced by a more sophisticated coil-spring set-up in 1995. Curiously, there has been no automatic transmission on any Frontera.

Vital statistics

Engine:	1,998cc injected petrol four-cylinder, with 115bhp at 5,200rpm and 125lb.ft at 2,600rpm (127lb.ft at 2,800rpm from March 1995) (SWB only)
	or 2,410cc injected petrol four-cylinder, with 125bhp at 4,800rpm and 144lb.ft at 2,600rpm (LWB only, to March 1995)
	or 2,198cc injected petrol four-cylinder, with 136bhp at 5,200rpm and 149lb.ft at 2,600rpm (LWB only, from March 1995)
	or 2,260cc indirect-injection intercooled turbodiesel four-cylinder, with 100bhp at 4,200rpm and 158lb.ft at 2,200rpm (LWB only, to March 1995)
	or 2,772cc indirect-injection intercooled turbodiesel four-cylinder, with 113bhp at 3,600rpm and 178lb.ft at 2,100rpm (SWB and LWB, from March 1995)
Transmission:	Five-speed manual Selectable four-wheel drive Lockable front hubs; automatic as standard, manual type optional Optional limited-slip rear differential
Suspension:	Independent front suspension with wishbones, torsion bar springs and anti-roll bar Live rear axle with semi-elliptic leaf springs (to March 1995) or coil springs (from March 1995)
Steering:	Power-assisted as standard
Brakes:	Discs at the front; drums at the rear (to March 1995) or discs at the rear (from March 1995) Power assistance standard ABS optional (from March 1995)
Dimensions:	Wheelbase SWB 91.8in (2,330mm) LWB 108.7in (2,760mm) Length SWB 165.8in (4,207mm)

Despite some glaring shortcomings (which were largely eliminated in the 1995 revisions), the Fronteras have sold very well, ranking second only to the Land Rover Discovery in UK sales volumes. The only exception was the soft-top Sport model which was introduced early in 1994 and abandoned a year later because of poor sales.

		LWB 183.6in (4,708mm)
	Height	SWB 66.9in (1,698mm)
		LWB 67.6in (1,715mm)
	Width	SWB 70.1in (1,780mm)
		LWB 68.1in (1,728mm)
	Ground clearance	7.3in (185mm) to March '95
		8.1in (205mm) from March '95
	Weight	SWB 3,500lb (1,588kg)
		LWB petrol 5,280lb (2,395kg)
		LWB diesel 5,600lb (2,540kg)
Number of seats:	SWB 4/5	
	LWB 7	
Towing capacity:	SWB	4,400lb (2,000kg)
	LWB petrol	5,280lb (2,400kg)
	LWB turbodiesel	5,500lb (2,500kg)
Insurance rating:	Group 10	
Fuel consumption:	SWB petrol	23mpg
	SWB turbodiesel	35mpg
	LWB 2.2 pet	27mpg
	LWB 2.4 pet	20mpg
	LWB 2.3 turbodiesel	28mpg
	LWB 2.8 turbodiesel	33mpg
Top speed:	SWB petrol	97mph
	SWB turbodiesel	93mph
	LWB 2.2 pet	100mph
	LWB 2.4 pet	96mph
	LWB 2.3 turbodiesel	78mph
	LWB 2.8 turbodiesel	93mph
0–60mph:	SWB petrol	13.5sec
	SWB turbodiesel	14.9sec
	LWB 2.2 pet	12.7sec
	LWB 2.4 pet	16.5sec
	LWB 2.3 turbodiesel	19.5sec
	LWB 2.8 turbodiesel	15.5sec

Character summary

The SWB three-door Sport versions are, of course, the weekend recreational off-roaders aimed at younger buyers; the LWB five-door Estate models are by contrast the family models. Both are roomy vehicles, although space in the rear of the SWB types is not as good as it looks.

The dashboard has a rather old-fashioned and unattractive appearance, although black plastic instead of the original grey improved it on post-1995 models. Equipment levels are generally quite good in both SWB and LWB models. Pre-1995 LWB Estates had an awkward swing-away spare-wheel carrier at the rear, which earned them few friends and was modified to a more convenient design for later models.

The Frontera aims to be as car-like as possible, while retaining the chunky and solid appeal of a 4x4. Its driving position is very car-like, although it seems strangely unsuited to a four-wheel drive vehicle.

Performance summary

The post-1995 models are very much superior to the earlier types as driver's vehicles: even the 2-litre petrol engine in the later Sport has better pulling power. The 2.4-litre petrol engine in early Estates is frustratingly lacking in urge and the 2.3-litre turbodiesel a plodder; the 2-litre engine in the early SWB models is only adequate.

Anyone seeking a rare 4x4 will find one in the soft-top version of the Frontera Sport, which was introduced in 1994 but withdrawn within a year because of limited demand.

The hardtop-bodied Frontera Sport has been considerably more popular; this is the Isuzu-engined 2.8 TD version introduced in 1995.

Handling is quite car-like on all Fronteras, but the steering on pre-1995 models is rather vague; later types are much better. Ride comfort is good on the early Estates, but the pre-1995 SWB models suffer from pitch and bounce; the coil-spring suspension introduced in 1995 both improved the ride of the Estates and smoothed out the SWB models' irritatingly lively ride.

Off-road, the SWB Frontera is inevitably a better performer than the LWB model, and the later 2.8-litre turbodiesel model gives the best account of itself. However, the wide tyres fitted as standard (mainly for the sake of appearances) can cause a lack of directional control on hard, rutted ground. The Frontera's independent front suspension is perhaps its most serious drawback, however, and the transmission protection plate fitted as standard makes clear that its makers are well aware of the risk of grounding.

Reliability, weaknesses, spares
All models of Frontera have shown themselves to be reliable vehicles. No consistent weaknesses have become apparent, although there are irritating design faults on the pre-1995 models – in particular, the LWB versions' swingaway spare-wheel carrier.

Spares are readily obtainable through Vauxhall dealers, and are reasonably priced.

Key specification changes in the UK
1991 (Oct):   Range introduced to UK
1993 (Aug):   Electric windows and heated mirrors standardized on SWB models

169

| 1994 (Mar): | Soft-top option introduced for SWB; retro-fit leather option announced for LWB |
| 1995 (Feb): | Revised engines introduced: 2.2-litre petrol replaced 2.4-litre, 2.8-litre turbodiesel replaced 2.3-litre, and 2-litre petrol improved; turbodiesel option for SWB; suspension, braking and steering upgrades; facia colour changed to black |

Nomenclature

Diamond	October 1993 limited edition (750 petrol, 750 turbodiesel), based on LWB models, with Spectral Blue metallic paint, grey leather upholstery, stainless steel nudge bar and side steps, fog and driving lamps; Dawes mountain bike included as standard
Estate	LWB models
Glacier	October 1994 special edition, based on LWB models, with Diamond Black, Satin Red or Velvet Green paint, colour-keyed front style bar, alloy wheels and side steps and special interior trim in cloth or leather
Nautilus	May 1994 special edition, based on LWB models, with alloy wheels, Nautilus blue pearlescent paint, side steps and colour-keyed front protection bar
Sport	SWB models
Sport S	High-line SWB models, from March 1995

Resale values

Fronteras are strong sellers and are much in demand on the used-car market. Residuals are strong, but values of the early models are likely to be weakened when examples of the much-improved 1995-specification types come onto the secondhand market in quantity. High specifications are particularly prized, but the unloved (and rare) soft-top Sport may not be a good long-term bet.

Club information

At the 1994 British International Motor Show, Vauxhall announced their new Off-Road Club. Vauxhall dealers hold application forms and further information.

Further reading

All pre-'95 models:	*International Off-Roader*, December 1991
	Off Road and 4 Wheel Drive, March 1993
	International Off-Roader, May 1994
All post-'95 models:	*International Off-Roader*, May 1995
Sport:	*Off Road and 4 Wheel Drive*, November 1992
	Autocar and Motor, July 21, 1993
	Off Road and 4 Wheel Drive, October 1993
LWB 2.3 turbodiesel:	*Autocar and Motor*, October 30, 1991
	Diesel Car, February 1992
	International Off-Roader, April 1993

VAUXHALL MONTEREY

Background

The Vauxhall Monterey is neither more nor less than a rebadged second-generation Isuzu Trooper, imported to the UK under an agreement between General Motors' Vauxhall subsidiary and the Japanese Isuzu company in which GM holds an interest. The Monterey was introduced alongside the strong-selling Trooper (imported by a separate company) in 1994 and will completely replace it on the UK market by 1997.

For the time being, the Monterey models are differentiated from their Trooper equivalents by specification levels: the Vauxhalls are rather better equipped and have higher price tags, mainly to help distance them from Vauxhall's other rebadged Isuzus, the Fronteras.

Vital statistics

Engine: 3,165cc injected 24-valve V6 petrol, with 174bhp at 5,200rpm and 192lb.ft at 3,750rpm
or 3,059cc four-cylinder turbodiesel, with 113bhp at 3,600rpm and 192lb.ft at 2,000rpm

---

The Monterey RS is Vauxhall's equivalent of the short-wheelbase Isuzu Trooper with additional equipment, including these five-spoke alloy wheels.

171

Transmission:	Five-speed manual or four-speed automatic (with petrol engine only) Selectable four-wheel drive Automatic freewheeling front hubs Limited-slip differential in the rear axle	
Suspension:	Independent front suspension, with twin wishbones and torsion bar springs; live rear axles with coil springs	
Steering:	Power-assisted as standard	
Brakes:	Ventilated discs front and rear, with standard power assistance ABS standard	
Dimensions:	Wheelbase	SWB 91.7in (2,330mm)
		LWB 108.6in (2,760mm)
	Length	SWB 178.9in (4,545mm)
		LWB 162in (4,115mm)
	Height	72in (1,830mm)
	Width	69in (1,752mm)
	Ground clearance	SWB 8.5in (215mm)
		LWB 8.3in (210mm)
	Weight	SWB petrol 3,954lb (1,794kg)
		SWB diesel 4,140lb (1,878kg)
		LWB petrol 4,140lb (1,878kg)
		LWB diesel 4,372lb (1,983kg)
Number of seats:	SWB 5 LWB 5; 7 optional	
Towing capacity:	6,614lb (3,000kg)	
Insurance rating:	Group 13	
Fuel consumption:	SWB petrol	11–21 mpg
	SWB turbodiesel	17–27 mpg
	LWB petrol	11–21 mpg
	LWB turbodiesel	17–27 mpg
Top speed:	SWB petrol	105mph
	SWB turbodiesel	94mph
	LWB petrol	105mph
	LWB turbodiesel	94mph
0–60mph:	SWB petrol	11.5sec
	SWB turbodiesel	16.6sec
	LWB petrol	11.5sec
	LWB turbodiesel	16.6sec

The Monterey LTD mirrors the long-wheelbase version of the Isuzu Trooper, but again is adorned with a higher level of standard equipment in an effort to distance the two ranges as much as possible. The choice of power unit is between the 3.2-litre 24-valve V6 petrol engine with either five-speed manual or four-speed automatic gearbox and the 3.1-litre four-cylinder turbodiesel with manual transmission only.

Character summary

As with the Trooper, the three-door SWB Monterey is designed for younger buyers than the five-door LWB family estate. Both vehicles benefit from a more characterful exterior than the Trooper, with five-spoke alloy wheels; the LWB models also have a rubbing-strip which adds definition to their slab sides. Interiors are as bland as those of the Trooper, but the wood-and-leather trim on top-specification Diamond models does improve the ambience.

The Monterey tries hard to feel more like a car than a 4x4, and in general it succeeds. However, the rather upright driving position is most unlike a car's, and the LWB models offer considerably more interior room than a conventional saloon-derived estate. Both petrol and turbodiesel LWB Montereys make powerful and stable tow vehicles.

Performance summary

Both petrol and turbodiesel engines give very good road performance. Ride quality is good, although there is some wallow if the Monterey is pushed hard.

The steering can feel vague at speed, and the brakes seem rather remote, although their stopping power is beyond question.

Off-road, the SWB models are, of course, more agile than their LWB relatives. However, neither type of Monterey is more than adequate in demanding conditions, mainly because of their independent front suspension and the road-biased torque delivery of their engines.

Reliability, weaknesses, spares
There is no reason to think that the Monterey will show a less impressive reliability record than its excellent Isuzu-badged equivalents. Build quality of all models is to a very high standard and durability will no doubt also prove exemplary.

Spares are readily available through the large countrywide Vauxhall dealer network.

Key specification changes in the UK
1994 (May):   Range introduced to UK market

Nomenclature
Diamond   High-line LWB models, with two-tone paint, leather and wood trim, stainless steel tread plates, air conditioning, retractable load cover and load safety nets
LTD   LWB models
RS   SWB models

Resale values
The Monterey has not yet been on sale long enough for a resale value pattern to become established. However, the range is likely to have reasonably firm residuals.

Club information
At the 1994 British International Motor Show, Vauxhall announced their new Off-Road Club, intended for owners of Montereys and Fronteras. Vauxhall dealers hold application forms and further information.

Further reading
All models: *International Off-Roader*, June 1994
LWB turbodiesel: *Diesel Car*, November 1994

TOO NEW, TOO FEW...

New four-wheel drive models are appearing all the time; inevitably some of them were too new to have filtered down to the used-vehicle market by the time this book went to press. For completeness, however, brief details are included on these last two pages.

JEEP GRAND CHEROKEE

The Jeep Grand Cherokee was announced in the USA during 1992 as a competitor in the luxury four-wheel drive estate market. Its sleek and stylish body greatly enhances its visual appeal and its 215bhp, 5.2-litre V8 petrol engine gives it outstanding road performance.

Chrysler Jeep UK imported some left-hand drive examples during 1994 and the vehicle was expected to go on sale in right-hand drive form during the course of 1995.

The first examples of the Jeep Grand Cherokee 5.2 V8 Limited arrived in the UK in 1994 in left-hand-drive form.

KIA SPORTAGE

The Kia Sportage is a Korean-built 4x4 which comes as a stylish three-door SWB model or a compact five-door LWB. Engines include a Mazda 2.2-litre diesel and a pair of 2-litre petrol types, one with 16 valves. The first imports, during 1995, were of well-equipped five-door models; three-door models are expected in 1996.